Robotic Process Automation
and Risk Mitigation:

The Definitive Guide

Best Wishes

Robotic Process Automation and Risk Mitigation:

The Definitive Guide

Mary C. Lacity
and
Leslie P. Willcocks

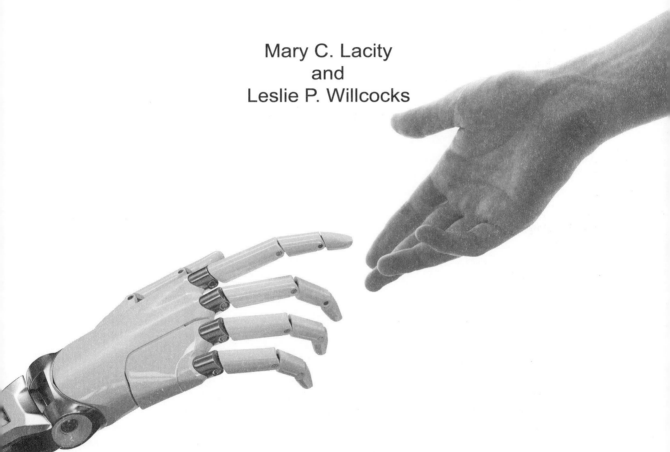

SB Publishing
United Kingdom

A 'SB Publishing' book
www.sbpublishing.org

Cover design:
Nick Sample
www.nicksample.com

Cover images:
The Prodigal Son by Giorgio de Chirico, Italian, 1888-1978
1965, oil on canvas © DACS 2017

Authors:
Mary C. Lacity and Leslie P. Willcocks
www.roboticandcognitiveautomation.com

Published in 2017 by:
SB Publishing
60 Loxley Road
Stratford-upon-Avon
Warwickshire CV37 7DR
United Kingdom
Tel: +44(0)1789 267124

A CIP catalogue record for this book is available from the British Library
ISBN 978-0-9956820-3-0

Printed and bound in Malta by Latitude Press Ltd.

Contents

Contents

Figures

Tables

Preface

Achieving the potential of an emerging technology like RPA (Robotic Process Automation) often starts by asking the right questions. It requires taking a step back from the hype and even misinformation, which can be difficult.

Today we have a 'Tower of Babel', with people talking about scripting tools, software robots, cognitive computing, machine learning, artificial intelligence, automatic content generators, all loosely defined while often being used interchangeably. We need to be very precise in our definitions and clear about what each technology enables users to do.

That is why this Guide is so important. It provides a framework not only for mitigating RPA risks but also for helping managers deliver value to shareholders, customers, and employees without risk. This recent effort by Mary and Leslie looks at the technology in a very holistic way. It debunks many myths including RPA being a 'job killer', that automation is merely about ROI or that all RPA solutions are created equal. It reflects on the digital transformations that many companies have embarked on looking to drive innovation, improve customer service, and stay competitive with RPA.

The lessons and knowledge derived from in-depth case studies, interviews, and surveys on organizational adopters of RPA and Cognitive Automation (CA) are all here. The methodology and framework walk you through the pitfalls, challenges and best practices for aligning RPA with company strategy, work and process design, employee motivation, messaging, IT infrastructure and overall management. Even more importantly is how this Guide closes the 'loop' by highlighting how RPA experiences need to be built over time and fed back into organizational learning.

Another key finding in these pages is just how powerful and disruptive RPA software can be. As one of the founders of Blue Prism, our company has literally pioneered and 'invented' the category of RPA. We always knew our technology was disruptive but you can never be too blasé about ROI numbers. The research is based on scores of client organizations that have adopted RPA as well as multiple RPA advisers and providers. Adopters include some long-standing and marquee Blue Prism customers. The research reveals that one-year returns on investments (ROI) for RPA solutions ranged from 30 percent at the low end to triple digits at the highest level.

This goes a long way to explaining why the RPA market is exploding. By the end of 2016, conservative estimates have the RPA and Cognitive Automation (CA) market undergoing an astronomical annual growth rate of around 47 percent culminating in a $22 billion plus market by 2024.

But RPA is not a simple silver bullet or cure-all. Automation has broad ramifications and needs both C-suite and IT support. It crosses so many disciplines, departments and lines of command. It is more of a digital transformation and people need to be trained and motivated so that they are committed and competent to configure, deploy and gain benefits from the RPA tools. This key finding also reveals how Blue Prism was built from the ground up as an ongoing collaboration between business leaders and IT management.

In order to mitigate risk, RPA experience needs to be built over time and fed into organizational learning. Experienced project managers and team members are required, while business leaders and users, and their knowledge and support, must be fully engaged.

In the end, if companies are using automation strategically, employees should benefit. This means using automation tools to automate very repetitive and boring work, freeing up internal staff to work on tasks that are more varied, complex, and interesting. It also means going beyond ROI numbers and seeing it as an opportunity to improve customer experience and employee satisfaction. Again, automation needs to address multiple stakeholders to be successful and should never be treated as a quick fix.

We are at an interesting inflection point as a society, which will only see the impact of automation accelerate. I have enjoyed reading this Guide because it asks the right questions not only about using a technology, but also about the future of work. Welcome to the brave new world of automation.

David Moss, Blue Prism, Chief Technology Officer & Co-Founder

Acknowledgements

'Robotic Process Automation and Risk Mitigation: The Definitive Guide' by Mary C. Lacity and Leslie P. Willcocks is one of the outputs delivered from a much more extensive research program covering Robotic Process Automation and Cognitive Automation. We are delighted to express our immense thanks and appreciation to all the customers, providers, and advisors interviewed for this research. We also acknowledge and thank Blue Prism for their participation and support of this work.

Authors' Foreword:
The Risk Navigation Challenge

"There are three routes to failure - gambling, sex and technology. Of these, the first is the quickest, the second the most pleasurable, but technology is the most certain." **Georges Pompidou**

"Luck is unreliable." **A. Ripley**

This guide is the product of a two and a half year collaboration between the researchers at the University of Missouri, St. Louis and the Department of Management at the London School of Economics and Political Science. Our overall aim has been to explore and understand digital technologies and their relationship to, and impact on, the future of work. In that regard we are pursuing parallel research into the potential impact of:

> **S**ocial media,
> **M**obile technologies,
> **A**nalytics and Big Data,
> **C**loud services,
> **B**lockchains,
> **R**obotics,
> **A**utomation of knowledge work,
> the **I**nternet-of-Things, and
> **D**igital Fabrication,

which we call SMAC/BRAID. The overall research program, begun some five years ago, is global, and covers multiple industrial and service sectors. We are aiming to understand how the major digital technologies, impact and are shaped by organizations, and how work is performed.

Within this remit, in late 2014, we identified the potentially explosive impact of ongoing developments in robotics and the automation of knowledge work. Our aim is to assess the current and long-term effects of business services automation on client organizations. While using software to automate/augment work is not a new idea, recent interest in service automation has certainly escalated, with the introduction of new technologies including Robotic Process Automation (RPA) and Cognitive Automation (CA) tools. This has brought further focus to our research (see Appendix A: Research Methodology). Looking just at RPA and CA, we found many potential adopters of these new types of service automation tools were skeptical about the claims surrounding their promised business value. Potential adopters need exposure to actual detailed client adoption stories. Mature adopters want to learn about advanced practices and benchmark their capabilities. Academic researchers can help educate potential and mature adopters, by bringing research rigour and objectivity to the process of examining actual RPA and CA implementations in client firms. This is achieved by assessing what the software can and cannot yet do, by identifying risks, and by extracting learnings on realizing business value.

By the end of 2015 the Robotic Process Automation and Cognitive Automation market was quite small, barely making $2 billion in revenues for RPA providers. By the end of 2016 this had increased some 68 percent with conservative sources estimating a compound annual growth rate of around 47 percent thereafter, adding up to a $22 billion plus market by 2024. One only needs to add in the growing army of advisory, consulting and implementation specialist firms, who also look to add and reap value, to see that a service industry is in the making. All this before business deployment of CA seriously takes off. From our client survey evidence, this was set to do so during the latter part of 2017.

Our initial response had been to study the success stories, challenges and hard won lessons from RPA experiences. The accumulated research was published in working papers throughout 2016 and in our comprehensive book *Service Automation Robots and The Future of Work* (SB Publishing, England), which also addresses how automation would impact on the future of work. In the course of our follow-up research stretching into 2017, and also embracing CA, it became clear that risk perception on RPA, let alone CA, remained poor. A lot more informed and considered evidence was needed for practitioners to make automation decisions. Assured by effective precedents and actions, they would be able to act with confidence thereafter. We found two things:

Firstly, there was no comprehensive analysis of the risks engendered by pursuing service automation. But RPA adoption was growing rapidly throughout 2016-17, and even global organizations were looking concernedly, sometimes desperately, for all the knowledge and experience they could muster.

Secondly, we found ourselves sitting on a very rich, and growing, research database that could answer the persistent questions we received on this subject, whenever we presented our work. After carrying out additional follow-up studies specifically focused on risk, and collecting more case studies to add to our existing research base, we analysed the data. **The result is this Guide**.

Risk is understood here as the probability of something happening, multiplied by the resulting cost or benefit if it does. We are particularly interested in **(1)** the likelihood of an adverse event occurring, **(2)** the size and impact of that adverse event in RPA deployments, and **(3)** how the risk hazard can be mitigated, and possibly converted into a favourable outcome.

In RPA, what is at risk comprises the multiple benefits or 'triple win' we describe in Chapter 2. The risk incurred when deploying advanced information and communication technologies (ICTs) in and across organizations is an absolutely fascinating, under-researched and also under-managed area. We have been studying risks in ICT projects for over 20 years and our risk and ICT framework suggests there are multiple sources of risk, some of them not immediately obvious (see Figure A1). Our evidence is that this framework applies also to RPA implementations in contemporary organizations.

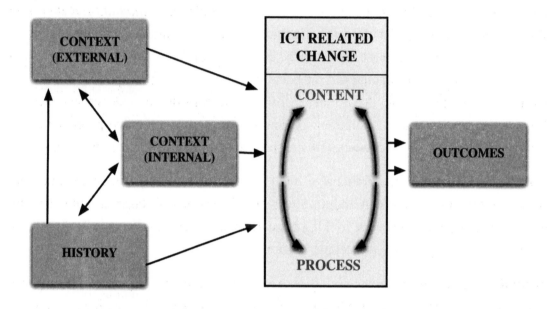

Figure A1: Framework for Diagnosing ICT (and RPA) Risk
(Source: Willcocks and Griffiths[1])

The direct technical/technology and project risks ('content' and 'process' in Figure A1) themselves receive the most attention and tend to be the most managed. Unfortunately, there are many other non-technology (and technology) risk sources. These can be environmental 'external context', to do with organizational history (e.g. ICT failures in the past), and/or arise from 'internal context' e.g. organizational, decisional, behavioural, and how strategy, technology, structure, process and people interact and (mis)align. New risks are added over time. Moreover, our research has shown that risks interconnect, creating hidden and high risks, sometimes systems threatening, from seemingly isolated, manageable sources of risk.

Historically, we have discovered three critical, recurring, sources of risk when deploying ICTs, and these, we find, apply directly to the deployment of service automation tools. **Firstly**, project management disciplines need to be in place. **Secondly**, low experience with the generic technology, and its subsequent deployment in a specific context by client and supplier/IT specialists, increases risk. **Thirdly**, the larger the size of deployment the more risk rises, sometimes exponentially (Willcocks and Griffiths, 1998)[2].

Of these, we argue in the Guide, project management should be a core organizational management capability, and RPA and CA deployments require the same level of project management discipline and attention as any other technology, business or organizational project. The low experience with the technology is an interesting one with RPA/CA as we shall see in Chapter 1. Some RPA tools are designed to be much more user friendly, less invasive, and easier to deploy and scale than others. Some RPA tools need much more work by IT developers to get them up and working with existing enterprise systems. An early 2017 count found there were over 39 suppliers badging their products as "RPA". Depending on the choice of tool, low experience with the technology can engender low risk or high risk, and in each "RPA" tool case, probably different risks. The third factor—size of RPA project—definitely relates to risk. Many of the earlier RPA projects we researched (for example Telefónica O2 and npower) were relatively small, and the organizations evolved their RPA capability over time. During 2016 and 2017, we saw much more ambitious, even global projects being initiated, with accelerated time-scales, and covering multiple units. These experienced higher levels of cumulative and interconnected risk, but with higher projected payoffs, and had to take on further change management and program management practices.

This leads to an initial, generic, two-part risk profiling framework we have adapted from our earlier studies of ICT-based business projects in light of our RPA/CA research findings. The framework is designed to sensitize the reader to the complexity of risk, and the importance of carrying out regular and comprehensive analysis. In later chapters we will detail specific risks engendered in RPA, and to some extent CA deployments across the service automation life-cycle.

External Context

Looking at Figure A2, external pressures to adopt service automation tools are growing due to heightened competitive rivalry - *Are competitors adopting RPA?* Cost issues, and the potential multiple business benefits possible, in the face of rising amounts of work produced by the data explosion and growth in regulation and audit. All this may lead to organizations short-circuiting normal wariness with new technologies. The relative newness of the technology and software to organizations and the dynamism of the RPA marketplace, i.e. growing number of competing suppliers, advisors, partners. Plus variations in products and services, together with rising skills shortages, could engender significant risk in specific RPA deployments.

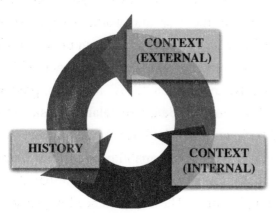

- Environmental pressures
- Newness/maturity of technology
- Supplier/consultant markets
- Competitor use of RPA/CA

- Organizational characteristics
  - strategy structure, reward system, human resources, management
- Employee relations context
- IT infrastructure and management
- Changing business neeeds

- IT/RPA success/failure
- Relevant IT/RPA experience
- Organizational

Figure A2: RPA/CA Risk Profiling
(Adapted from Willcocks and Griffiths[3])

Organizational History

A history of success or failure with technology can create risks, and the perception of risk. In some organizations a history of technology failure can create lack of support and engagement with subsequent technologies like RPA/CA. On the other hand, a history of past ICT success can make organizations less cautious and more over-confident with RPA/CA. Where the IT function traditionally 'owns' software products, the RPA can become over-identified as just another IT tool. The importance of seeing RPA automation as a business project with business benefits, needing high business engagement, and even location within business operations, may be lost to the organization. We have also seen RPA tool selection taken over by IT specialists, who tend to choose IT self-development kits in their own image, thus eschewing the advantage of selecting more user-friendly RPA tools (see Chapter 1).

Internal Context

In most of the RPA deployments we study, RPA is treated as a business project, with ownership by business operations. This may be very sensible but it is critical then, during the deployment, to take into account all the organizational attributes that can impact on success. As Figure A2 illustrates, failing to align RPA tool use with strategy, structure, work and process design, employee motivation and messaging, IT infrastructure and management and changing business needs, will engender cumulative risk.

Content

On content, our findings on ICT implementations pass directly into RPA deployments we have studied, see Figure A3. As project size and complexity increase, so does risk. As technical uncertainty, i.e. How does it work and in what context? and definitional uncertainty, i.e. What does it do and what do we require? increase, risk builds. As the number of business units affected increases, risk escalates, e.g. shared global services.

Process

Historically ICT project failure is most frequently related to an overfocus on technical efficiency and outcomes, and an under-resourcing of process issues. We observe the same pattern in the RPA projects we have studied. Figure A3 points to the major issues. People need to be trained and motivated so that they are committed and competent to configure, deploy and gain benefits from the RPA tools. RPA experience needs to be built over time and fed into organizational learning. Experienced project managers and team members are required, while business leaders and users with their knowledge and support, must be fully engaged. Without these, and we have observed these omissions in several RPA deployments, risk accumulates. Increasingly we are seeing into 2017 higher labor turnover in RPA-specific roles, as staff get lured away to other client organizations, or adviser, consultancy and service partner firms.

RPA/IT RELATED CHANGE

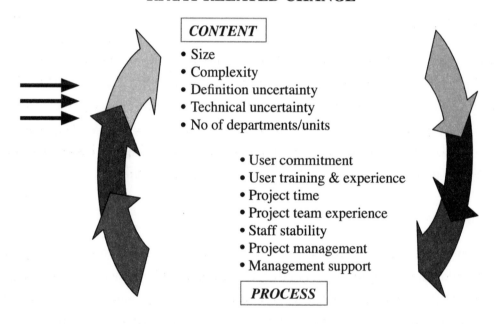

CONTENT

- Size
- Complexity
- Definition uncertainty
- Technical uncertainty
- No of departments/units

- User commitment
- User training & experience
- Project time
- Project team experience
- Staff stability
- Project management
- Management support

PROCESS

Figure A3: RPA Risk Profiling
(Source: Adapted from Willcocks and Griffiths)[4]

Risk and Perception

Before we proceed with our analyses of material risks arising in RPA deployments, and how to manage these, we need to highlight a point Sandman[5] makes in his work on risk as a social construction. He offers the formula:

RISK = HAZARD + OUTRAGE

As he argues, the key fact about risk communication is the very low correlation between a risk's 'hazard' and its 'outrage', i.e. how much harm it's likely to do and how upset it's likely to make people. What we are doing in this Guide combines a number of objectives. One task is 'precaution advocacy', where hazard is high and perception/outrage low, and we are alerting insufficiently informed or upset people to serious risks. The eight sets of risks we identify in Chapter 3 fall into the medium to high risk category.

A second task, where there is low hazard but high outrage, is 'outrage management', reassuring upset people that risks are smaller than they think or feel. An example is the high alarm and 'outrage' with which the automation and the future of work debate is conducted in the media. This may alarm many employees and organizations, but is fed all too often by studies replete with weak data, speculation, poor assumptions, neglect of important factors, the omission of job creation, mistaken beliefs in the speed with which technologies can get deployed, and underestimation of the distinctive qualities and value humans bring to work. We do little 'outrage management' in this guide but provide a detailed critique of the conduct of the automation and the future of work debate in our earlier book.

A third task is to address the likelihood of adverse outcomes and missed potential benefits, by detailing countervailing actions needed to take the RPA journey in a more positive direction. This is achieved in Chapters 3 through 9. We offer across the RPA lifecycle 30 action principles that keep the RPA project on course, and get the organization to the point where it can integrate automation initiatives, and establish an **Automation Center of Excellence.** Let our risk navigation challenge begin.

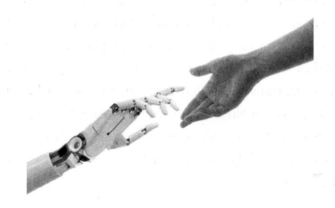

Chapter 1

Introduction to Robotic Process Automation

"We have seen a tendency to separate risks into rigid silos—operational risk, market risk, credit risk and so on. But what we have found is that major shocks and problems do not come that way."

Richard J. Herring

The latest breed of service automation tools and platforms span a variety of capabilities. The proliferation of terms and jargon has been called a 'Tower of Babel', with people talking about scripting tools, software robots, cognitive intelligence, machine intelligence, artificial intelligence, automatic content generators, cognitive learning technologies, autonomic platforms, and cognitive computing, as some common examples. To help make sense of this landscape, we classified these tools along a service automation continuum, anchoring one end of the scale as the 'realm of RPA' and the other end of the scale as the 'realm of cognitive automation' (see Figure 1.1).

We define the 'realm of RPA' as software that automates tasks currently performed by a human, by following rules to process structured data. RPA tools produce a single correct answer. Although many software firms are now calling their products "RPA", for us RPA has two additional features:

First, the software does not require traditional IT programming skills but instead the software is 'configured' through an easy-to-use design interface. This feature means that business professionals rather than IT professionals can configure the software to perform the automation.

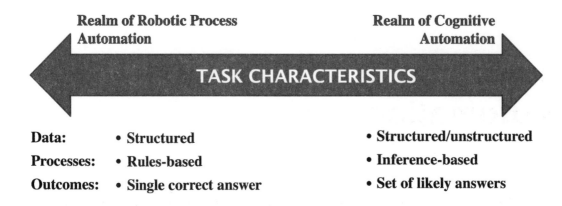

Data:	• Structured	• Structured/unstructured
Processes:	• Rules-based	• Inference-based
Outcomes:	• Single correct answer	• Set of likely answers

Figure 1.1: The Service Automation Continuum
(Source: Adapted from Lacity and Willcocks (2016)[6])

Second, the software is non-invasive by interacting with existing systems through the user interfaces, typically by assigning the RPA software a user ID and password. This feature means that the software is enterprise safe because it sits on top of enterprise systems and doesn't create, replace, or further develop expensive platforms.

As an important caveat, not all RPA products are the same. Tools differ, for example, by deployment approach—some tools are deployed on desktops or servers, and others are cloud-based (see Figure 1.2). Additionally, some IT toolkits that are becoming increasingly user-friendly are marketed as RPA. Different RPA tools will create different risks, even in similar contexts, so it is important for organizational adopters to pick the RPA approach that matches their business strategy, as discussed in Chapter 5.

On the opposite end of the service automation continuum is the 'realm of cognitive automation' (CA), which we define as tools designed to automate or augment tasks that use inference-based processes on unstructured (and structured) data to produce a set of likely outcomes or interpretations. IBM's Watson is considered the übermachine in this space. But again, the automation landscape is a continuum. Cognitive virtual agents, for example, process unstructured data but also follow rules to produce single outcomes for task execution. IPsoft's Amelia is one such example.[7]

Figure 1.2: Variety of RPA Tools

We have done in-depth case studies, interviews, and surveys on organizational adopters of RPA and CA and we now have a good understanding of both the RPA and CA realms. In this guide, we focus on the realm of RPA, which we describe as 'today's technology'. **It makes sense to focus on RPA because most organizations in our case studies and surveys report more mature and higher adoption rates for RPA than CA tools.** (In contrast to RPA, most organizations we are studying are still experimenting with CA or are just beginning to deploy CA services. Thus, in early 2017, we called the realm of CA 'tomorrow's technology' for most organizations.)

To date, our research shows that best practice organizations gain a 'triple win' from RPA: a win for shareholders, a win for customers, and a win for employees. This triple win, covered in Chapter 2, shows "The RPA art of the possible", that is, what organizations can achieve if they can mitigate the risks identified in Chapter 3. What differentiates successful RPA from mediocre RPA initiatives? Our research suggests that successful organizations identified and mitigated risks with a number of management practices, which we call 'action principles'[8] (see Table 1.1). Action principles are similar to best practices in that both seek to share knowledge from prior experiences. But here is where they differ: whereas 'best practices' imply that mimicry will always produce similar results, action principles recognize that context matters. Managers are

Risk Categories	Major Risks	Action Principles to Mitigate Risks
Strategy	Missing value by not understanding the triple-win, by thinking too small and short-term, by delegating too low in the organization, by funding too little, or by viewing automation only as an opportunity to cut costs. Damaging reputation if messaged as a way to cut jobs	1. Conceive of RPA as an enabler of a larger business strategy 2. Cultural adoption by the C-suite 3. Consider RPA for more than just cost savings 4. Decide who is best to 'own' the automation program
Sourcing Selection	Missed value or excessive costs by choosing the wrong sourcing model or wrong advisers/partners, or right ones too late. Getting locked into tools or BPO providers	5. Use credible advisory firms to bridge gaps in client knowledge 6. Incentivize BPO providers to share the benefits of automation
Tool Selection	Choosing the wrong tool(s), too many tools, or bad tool(s)	7. Match tool capabilities with strategic objectives 8. Consider overall value of tool capabilities, not just price 9. Have IT help vet the software 10. Test tool capabilities with a controlled contest 11. Select a software provider with sound financial position and stable customers
Stakeholder Buy-In	Stakeholders ignore, stall, resist or derail the automation program	12. Involve IT from the start 13. Communicate the value of automation to employees 14. Promise no layoffs as a consequence of service automation; ratchet down headcount gradually instead 15. Select 'rising stars' for service automation projects 16. Redesign employee scorecards
Automation Launch	Initial projects fail technically, financially or politically	17. Select 'wow' projects based on impact to customers and employees 18. Build realistic business cases 19. Redesign human work for robotic work 20. Consider the Pareto Principle
Operations/ Change Management	The robots do not function as intended. As business rules evolve or IT interfaces change, organization fails to adapt RPA	21. Make sure the robots are work-ready 22. Manage the robotic workforce 23. Assign clear boundaries of responsibility
Road to Maturity	Automation momentum stalls from champions leaving, skills shortages, under-utilizing software robots. Integration issues emerge as new technologies are adopted.	24. Establish a Center of RPA Excellence 25. Rethink talent development for skills needed for an enterprise automation capabilities 26. Multi-skill the software robots 27. Reuse components to scale quickly and to reduce development costs 28. Continually improve existing automations 29. Integrate tools to automate services end-to-end 30. Establish a Center of Automation Excellence

Table 1.1: Risk Mitigation Framework

thoughtful agents that scrutinize 'best practices' derived from other people's learnings and decide whether practices need to be modified, or perhaps discarded.

In Table 1.1 we provide an overview of the content of Chapters 3 through 9 covering the major risks, and the action principles that can mitigate the likelihood of adverse events occurring. However, one does not usually take risks without expecting a return. There has to be a possible upside when organizations run a risk, to make incurring the risk worthwhile. In the next Chapter we point to the types of benefits firms are reporting from their RPA investments. The surprising news is that despite skepticism on the part of managers disappointed with several previous waves of IT investment, RPA has been turning out to be typically relatively cheap and quick to deploy, and has been providing multiple business benefits. The next chapter gives chapter and verse.

Chapter 2

The RPA Art of the Possible

"You'll always miss 100% of the shots you don't take."

Wayne Gretzky

We have documented several organizations that have achieved the triple-win for shareholders, customers, and most surprising of all, employees. Our book, ***Service Automation: Robots and the Future of Work***[9] covers the triple wins at the Associated Press, Telefónica O2, Xchanging, and many other companies. We have continued to study RPA adopters, and found other companies also achieving the triple win. Aggregating these findings, we have listed the specific benefits and sources of shareholder, customer, and employee value that RPA has delivered across case study companies (see Figure 2.1). What is interesting is that we are finding some organizations experiencing not just one or two but multiple business benefits from their RPA investments. How this can happen is the subject of this Guide.

2.1. Shareholder Value

Organizations in our study routinely delivered value to shareholders in terms of high returns on investment, operational efficiencies, improved compliance, improved scalability, and increased adaptability to changing requirements. As best practice organizations scaled and matured their RPA capabilities, a truly flexible workforce and a competitive advantage over rivals were delivered.

SHAREHOLDER VALUE	CUSTOMER VALUE	EMPLOYEE VALUE
♠ High first year ROIs ♠ Operational efficiencies ♠ Increased compliance ♠ Increased scalability ♠ Increased adaptability ♠ Workforce flexibility ♠ Competitive advantage	♠ Improved service quality ♠ Faster delivery of existing services ♠ Improved service consistency ♠ Round-the-clock availability ♠ New services online quickly ♠ Enhanced customer journeys	♠ More interesting work ♠ Learned new skills ♠ Increased employee satisfaction ♠ Enhanced reputation as an innovator

Figure 2.1: The RPA Art of The Possible: The 'triple-win'

High first year ROIs: One of the most astounding figures generated from our first thirteen RPA case studies was the reported one-year returns on investments (ROI) for RPA; the lowest one-year ROI was 30 percent and the highest one-year ROI was in the triple digits. Although we did not have access to each company's precise ROI formula, in general, organizations considered the costs of software licenses, training, consulting, and developing RPA cases against the financial benefits of FTE savings, or as is increasingly common, the value of the number of human hours saved after RPA. For example, one UK retailer returned 280,000 hours back to the business in 2016 (equal to 140 FTEs), of which 80,000 hours in savings were generated from new automations that year. 'Hours back to the business' became a key RPA performance metric. As of 2017, this retailer had 97 live RPA processes.

Operational efficiencies: 'Doing more work without hiring more staff' was a commonly reported operational efficiency. In particular, Global Business Services (GBS) were expected to take on higher service volumes without adding headcount. In other cases, GBS staff were so over-stretched before RPA that they had to take shortcuts. One example from our research was a GBS organization that only had enough human resources to validate about 15 percent of payroll. Humans focused only on the high-risk employees. After RPA, the entire payroll was validated and exceptions were passed to the humans for processing. The GBS head said,

> *"I can actually cover more work, get a better customer service outcome, and I can make life for my employees a lot better."*[10]

Increased compliance: When humans are trained to perform a service, variability will inevitably result. While the human factor can enhance a service, it also leads to the possibility of misinformation or lack of compliance with standards. RPA software robots execute precisely as configured to do so, thus compliance can increase after automation. One large bank reported 100 percent compliance and adherence to regulatory requirements after RPA, particularly with respect to Treating Customers Fairly (TCF).[11] We found organizations in closely regulated industries, including utilities, banks, telecoms and insurance companies, placing a high value on both speed to compliance, but then the accuracy, fast processing and audit trails produced.

Increased scalability: Organizations reported increased scalability, defined as the ease with which organizations can meet fluctuations in service demand, as a result of RPA. For example, when a new iPhone was released, Telefónica O2 added more software robots to process orders rather than hire hordes of temporary workers to meet the demand surge. In another example, an energy company re-used existing software robots to meet an unexpected government regulation to craft a bespoke letter to every commercial customer. The software robots completed the task in six weeks compared to the estimate of hiring 30 temporary human workers for three months.

Increased adaptability: RPA certainly improved adaptability, defined as the ease with which automations can be altered to accommodate new or changing process rules or data types. When humans are asked to learn a new business rule, everyone needs to be trained. In contrast, a new rule or data type has to be written only once for a software robot. (This presumes that the tool is enterprise RPA as we defined it in Chapter 1; one risk is that some RPA tools with a record feature might require starting over from scratch if one step in a process changes.)

Creates a flexible workforce: As organizations scale and mature their RPA capabilities, they begin to realize the value of a flexible workforce. The powerful combination of human-robot teams allows organizations to dynamically staff work units. Software robots can be multi-skilled (see action principle 26) to work on several teams. In one shared services organization, a software robot helps out an accounting team during the day and runs payroll at night.

Competitive advantage: When organizations view RPA as a critical enabler of their business/digital transformation strategy, RPA can deliver a competitive advantage over rivals. Some BPO providers and advisory firms became known for their RPA capabilities and were subsequently bought by larger competitors. Xchanging, a London-based business process and technology services provider, was bought by Computer Sciences Corp (CSC) in May of 2016.[12] Alsbridge, a leading RPA advisory firm, was bought by ISG in December of 2016.[13] Pundits cite both Xchanging's and Alsbridge's mature RPA capabilities as one reason they were so attractive to purchase.[14] For client organizations—in contrast to BPO providers and advisory firms that sell automated services—RPA combined with other tools enables organizational agility by allowing the organization to create and/or respond to new business or market opportunities. Another angle to competitive advantage is the customer value created, giving the company a service advantage over their rivals.

2.2. Customer Value

If organizations think of RPA only in terms of delivering shareholder value, they are missing an opportunity to add customer value and to differentiate services. The best practice organizations in our research selected automations that touched their customers. RPA commonly improved service quality by reducing errors, speeding service delivery, improving service consistency, and extending service availability to 24 hours. As best practice organizations scaled and matured their RPA capabilities, they started using RPA to bring new services online quickly and to enhance customer journeys.

Improved service quality: Service quality increases because software robots do not make mistakes, unlike humans who get bored, tired, and make errors on repeated tasks. In one financial services firm, the accuracy of notifications of losses on commercial motor insurance improved from 45 percent accuracy when humans input the data to 95 percent accuracy with RPA.[15]

Faster delivery of existing services: Services are delivered faster because software is faster than humans on rote tasks; in the case of the motor insurance notification, the turnaround speed was improved by 85 percent after RPA.[16] In other cases, such as at Xchanging and O2, service delivery times went from days to minutes when organizations moved rote tasks from human workers to software robots.

Improved service consistency: For the same reason RPA can increase compliance, RPA can improve service consistency; the software robots will execute services the same way each time. When one company was documenting processes in preparation for automation, it discovered that some human teams across the organization were using old processes. This company cited service consistency among the top three benefits of service automation.

Round the clock availability: Unlike humans, software robots do not sleep or eat. This benefits customers who get full service coverage. For one manager of Global Business Services (GBS) in a financial services firm, *"RPA doesn't sleep, does not go off sick, does not take vacation... the virtual, always-on workforce is something that we always dreamed of in the shared services industry in terms of follow the sun."* In addition to benefiting customers, employees and enterprises benefit because shift work and/or time zone coordination of dispersed human teams is avoided.

New services online quickly: RPA also brings down the cost of developing new services, allowing more services to be quickly deployed. One company's business operations staff used RPA to keep the customer abreast of every step in service delivery, which kept the customers informed and resulted in fewer calls to the service desk. Before RPA, the human staff did not have the bandwidth to send such notifications, and a request for IT to do the automation was given low priority. Another aspect of this value is the ability for business operations to prioritize and build their own services; in some organizations, IT-led automation projects took months or even years because of IT intake, prioritization, and resource allocation processes. In contrast, many RPA projects took just weeks to deliver, bringing new services to customers quickly.

Enhanced customer journeys: Some enterprises use software robots to strengthen customer journeys through the end-to-end processes of discovery, comparative shopping, considering, buying and retention. This requires thinking about a company's services from a customer's point of view, and subsequently prioritizing RPA projects that enhance the customer's experience. For example, a UK retail company wanted to support its customers after devastating flooding. The company used RPA software to identify the customers in the flood zone and sent them a message of support and sympathy, backed with a promise that customers' accounts would not be put into default for a late payment while the customer was recovering from the flood.

2.3 Employee Value

One of the most surprising findings from our research was the value RPA delivered to employees. Employees—those whose jobs were affected by RPA—commonly reported that their jobs became more interesting after RPA; they also commonly reported they enjoyed learning new skills and that RPA brought their teams accolades from senior managers.

More interesting work: We have coined the phrase "*RPA takes the robot out of the human*" to describe how RPA affects employees. In most of our case study companies, dreary tasks were done by the software robots, freeing the human employees to focus on tasks requiring judgment, problem-solving skills, creativity, empathy, and emotional intelligence. This was quite common in shared services organizations. Part of the job for many employees in shared services requires them to 'swivel' around their desks, just taking inputs from multiple sources, and cutting and pasting them into standardized forms before processing them and preparing outputs for systems of record. This is a reality in many shared services organizations, and very boring work indeed. After RPA took over these swivel chair tasks in our case companies, the employees spent more time on challenging, and higher value, tasks like developing new services, onboarding new departments, and resolving customer service issues. For example, at npower and Virgin Trains we saw automation taking over unexceptional meter reading and customer enquiries, freeing up staff to use their judgment, discretion and experience on more problematic cases.

Learn new skills: Employees in many of our case study companies were eager to learn the RPA tools. For many young workers in particular, software robots brought some excitement to the otherwise commonplace activities they performed, like processing claims or updating employee records. It was not unusual for employees to anthropomorphize their software robots by assigning them human names, depicting them as physical entities, inviting them to office parties, and even holding a contest for which team had the 'coolest' software robot. Figure 2.2 depicts examples from three companies. The female robot is "Poppy", the first software robot at Xchanging to be named and depicted by an employee; as more Xchanging teams adopted RPA, employees named their robots Sunny, Henry, etc. In another company, employees named all the robots "Dennis". The company had 40 software licenses, so names were Dennis 1, Dennis 2, through Dennis 40. Dennis 17 was known as a 'rascal': a robot that required more attention than the others. In the third company employees played on the name "Robert" and called their robots Robo Di Nero, Robo Martinez, Robo Downey Jr., etc.

Enhanced reputation as an innovator: Both individuals and teams became recognized as innovators within their organizations after RPA. Companies in our study praised employees in internal communications and some were promoted because of their contributions to service automation. One employee had spent most of her working life in a coffee shop and then came on board to work for a BPO firm. She was one of the first employees to help automate the repetitive tasks of her job. Her company asked us to interview her because she is considered an innovator. She described the RPA experience as follows:

> *"I'm in charge of our robot.... we talk about her as if she's a member of our team. She's removed pretty much 100 percent of human error so now our team is considered brilliant!"*

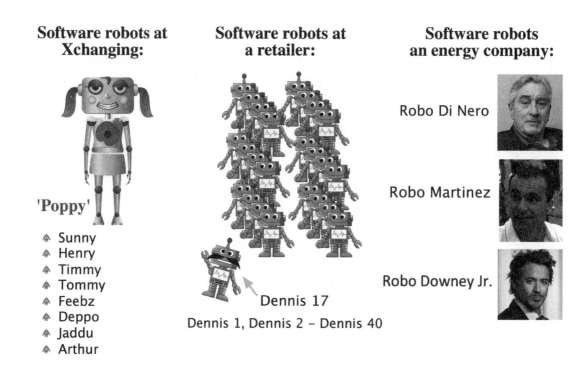

Software robots at Xchanging:	Software robots at a retailer:	Software robots an energy company:

'Poppy'
- Sunny
- Henry
- Timmy
- Tommy
- Feebz
- Deppo
- Jaddu
- Arthur

Dennis 17
Dennis 1, Dennis 2 – Dennis 40

Robo Di Nero

Robo Martinez

Robo Downey Jr.

Figure 2.2: Employees and their anthropomorphized software robots

Increased employee satisfaction: Many employees reported higher job satisfaction as a consequence of all of the above: liberation from dreary tasks, learning new skills, and becoming known as an innovator. Interestingly many employees were used to new technologies—they had advanced consumer IT at home—and welcomed technology investment that improved their work mix.

In summary, the vast majority of organizations in our study delivered value to shareholders, customers, and employees. Our initial research sample was biased in that we sought exemplars of RPA success stories. This does not mean, however, that their RPA journeys were without peril, and indeed some early pilots in organizations often highlighted key practices that were initially absent. From mid-2016 through 2017, we conducted additional interviews with clients, providers, and advisors to share war-stories of RPA projects or programs that struggled to deliver value to organizations. Combining the initial sample with follow-up research, we next catalog the risks that emerged from our analysis.

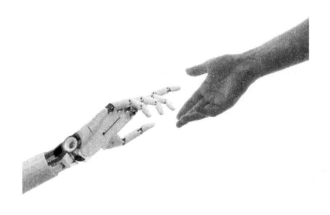

Chapter 3

RPA and Risks

"The first step in the risk management process is to acknowledge the reality of risk. Denial is a common tactic that substitutes deliberate ignorance for thoughtful planning." **Charles Tremper**

"Reality is that which, when you stop believing in it, doesn't go away."
Philip K. Dick

Service automation—like all organizational initiatives—is, in practice, fraught with risks. What might these risks be? We uncovered over 40 RPA risks from our interviews, which we organized into eight risk packets or categories: strategy, sourcing, tool selection, stakeholder buy-in, launch/project, operational/execution, change management, and maturity risks (see Figure 3.1).

RPA strategy risks. The greatest strategy risk involved missing the triple-win value of RPA by thinking too small, such as looking at automation as a tactical tool to cut costs on specific tasks within a department. Misunderstanding what RPA can do or burying the RPA initiative in a remote division also resulted in missed value for some companies. Not thinking strategically at all about automation, and seeing it as a tactical, even worse 'one-off' solution, seriously inhibited RPA potential. When organizations made these mis-steps, they usually under-resourced the RPA program, leading to very little value. Perhaps the worst damage occurs when automation is viewed as a way to cut jobs rather than change how work is done—that message can damage a company's reputation and exacerbate other risks, like stakeholder buy-in risks.

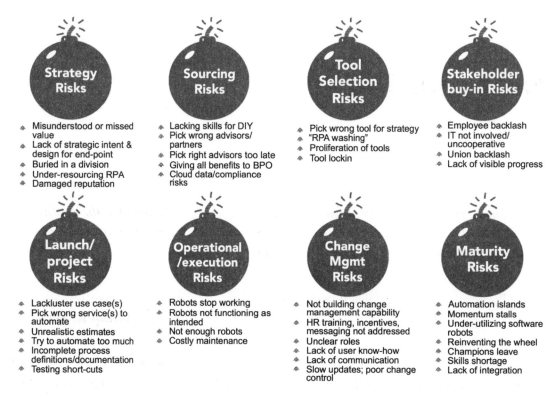

Figure 3.1: Major RPA Risks

RPA sourcing risks. Clients risk leaving value on the table or incurring excessive costs by choosing the wrong sourcing model. Some organizations tried to do everything themselves, but they lacked the needed skills to govern, develop, and execute robotic operations. In 2017 some organizations assumed more support from their RPA suppliers, who, in fact, were all to busy responding to fast rising demand elsewhere. Some organizations picked the wrong advisors or partners who claimed RPA expertise, but clients later discovered the partner was only "*a chapter ahead of us in the book*". One interviewee said "*Some partners don't train their people on RPA until they sell (i.e. get) the business—then it's mass panic, trying to train people and get them onsite in a week*". Some organizations picked the right advisors, but brought them on board too late, such as after the client had signed software licenses with a tool provider for a tool that did not match the client's needs. Some organizations relied on their traditional BPO providers for automation, but often too little value was passed to the client. Although cloud RPA is an emerging sourcing option, interviewees said that cloudsourcing brings extra data protection risks, particularly in highly regulated industries.

Tool selection risks. Because of the hype and confusion in the market place, clients risk choosing the wrong tool(s), too many, or bad tool(s). In 2016, about 39 tools were being sold as "RPA" and about 120 tools were being sold as some form of cognitive automation. Because the space is relatively new to many clients, it is difficult to assess the actual capabilities and suitability of these tools. Clients must be aware of hype and "RPA washing". The term "RPA washing" refers to the phenomenon of companies spending more resources on advertising and marketing, which claim to have new service automation capabilities, than actually building new automation capabilities. Cliff Justice, a partner at KPMG said, *"Absolutely, we see evidence of 'RPA washing'; we see real differences in capabilities across the tools and providers. This is a new market with emerging technologies. Some are more mature than others."*[17] Theo de Haas, Senior Business Partner Group Services, Royal DSM said, *"A lot of RPA vendors are really just doing screen scraping, which requires a lot of maintenance if you want to make changes. I think the biggest advantage that we have with Redwood is that everything is controlled by business rules. So my advice to companies that really want to do this is to do process automation and not screen automation. If you do this at the screen level, probably you'll wind up having even more problems that erode into your savings because you have huge maintenance on your hands."*[18]

Stakeholder buy-in risks. RPA initiatives require stakeholder buy-in from IT, employees, and customers, both internal and external. Some organizations experienced skepticism from IT staff that saw RPA as nothing new, replicating IT work and capability, and threatening system stability and security. In one case study, the employees belonged to a labor union that was quite capable of stalling or even derailing RPA. In another organization, some business users did not understand RPA and blamed anything that went wrong on the robots. For example, slow response time was blamed on RPA until the RPA team stopped the robots to prove that response times were slow because too many *humans* were logging in at the same time. In a further organization, the users claimed the robots went rogue, but the robots were doing exactly what the users told them to do. In other instances, RPA was so effective that no one noticed, and then complained there were no results. Most importantly, IT, employees and users are integral to the successful delivery of RPA, so RPA programs can stall, stumble, or fail without their active and early engagement.

Launch/project risks. Organizations have to mitigate several risks to prevent initial projects from failing technically, financially, and/or politically. Some companies picked projects in areas with the most headcount because they thought it would generate the most savings, but launch failed because the processes were constantly changing and required a lot of exception handling; it turned out those few hundred people were there for a reason. Failure also resulted from unrealistic project estimates, particularly for business cases that too aggressively aimed for immediate FTE savings. At one company, senior management mandated a headcount reduction within six months and presumed that automation was going to be the route. Everything went wrong: the RPA team did not get the resources it needed to build a successful RPA solution; the team was forced to quickly buy a tool based on the software vendor's sales promises, without spending the time and money to vet the tool's capabilities; the use cases naively assumed 100 percent automation, rather than following the Pareto principle of an 80/20 rule (see action principle 20). Shortcuts were taken, like sharing logon IDs and passwords, thus jeopardizing compliance and security. As the deadline approached, the organization violated the mythical man-month rule[19] when it hired external advisors to speed implementation. The advisors could only highlight the failures: to do the automations correctly would require a tremendous amount of rework.

Operational/execution risks. Operational risks happen when robots are moved from development into operations without proper verification or a proper operating model. One interviewee described this common mistake, *"Some organizations focus on when they can get the product and start training people. They don't define roles, everyone* *is wearing different hats, and the boundaries of responsibilities are blurred. Robots are put into production and people start running around like headless chickens, then the wheels come off.*" In the worst cases, the robots stop working or execute processes incorrectly. Some organizations did not have enough robots to handle volumes. Some organizations shoved robots into the production without any process redesign, which implemented RPA quickly, but resulted in high maintenance costs.

Change management risks. These link strongly with strategy, stakeholder buy-in, launch, as well as operational risks. Poor communication of the strategic intent— not actively seeking stakeholder buy-in, and not managing operational dynamics— together, these build cumulative multiple change management risks. Early adopters during the 2010-14 period tended to move slowly into RPA, not initially seeing its strategic potential, and only subsequently evolving into a mature capability. During late 2016-2017 we found more large organizations alerted to the need for a strategic approach to RPA and for automation generally. Whether in banking, other financial services, manufacturing, or focusing on shared services transformation, they wanted to achieve large-scale implementations quickly. However, this has introduced a whole new dimension to risk in terms of under-estimation of the change management activity required. At the strategy level and during launch we have seen initial weaknesses in establishing the project sponsor, a project champion, a multi-disciplinary team and project management disciplines. Change management capabilities (to keep strategy, processes, technology and people aligned throughout the RPA implementation process) have been under-resourced. Human resource issues (training and motivation, plus design of future work) have been inadequately addressed, all feeding into delays in building a mature capability and delivering the business benefits.

More operationally: Who is in charge of the robots? Software robots need to be reconfigured when business rules or data types change and when the interfaces to applications they touch change. When the change management roles between the business and IT were unclear, robots were not updated, causing them to function improperly or to stop running completely.

Maturity risks. When the previously identified risks were mitigated, companies frequently experienced the triple-win value from their first RPA deployments. Companies next aimed to expand RPA across their enterprises. However, a sustainable enterprise RPA capability can be impeded by a number of risks. Without good coordination, islands of automation proliferated, efforts were duplicated across divisions, and existing software robots were under-utilized. End-to-end processing remained an elusive goal as organizational, labour and process silos stood largely unchanged. And some organizations were fixated solely on RPA, and not the bigger picture of preparing for other automation advances and the next five years. Meanwhile the RPA champions at some organizations left the company; other companies reported a growing shortage of RPA skills, which slowed momentum.

In summary, there are many risks in any program of substance, including RPA programs. We aim to provide a realistic view of RPA by profiling these risks. Many organizations in our study certainly learned to minimize and even avoid these risks, even after they had initially charged down the wrong path. Organizations that eventually achieved the full promise of the RPA triple-win followed many of the practices we discuss next.

Chapter 4

Strategy Action Principles

"You may not be interested in strategy, but strategy is interested in you."

Leon Trotsky

We have argued that organizations should not develop an RPA strategy per se, but rather should identify how RPA can contribute to the enterprise's long-term goals.[20] To overcome the strategy risks of thinking too small and short-term (burying the RPA initiative in a remote division, or under-resourcing the RPA program), successful organizations conceived of RPA as an enabler of a larger business strategy, often times as part of a digital transformation strategy, achieved cultural adoption by the C-suite, expected many business benefits in addition to cost savings, and decided which organization was best to 'own' the automation program.

4.1. Conceive of RPA as an enabler of a larger business strategy

Service automation adopters with the best outcomes did not have an RPA strategy per se; they had a business strategy that was enabled, in part, by service automation. In our research, the business strategy depended upon the adopter's organizational context, such as whether adopters were from enterprise operations, Global Business Services, BPO providers, or advisory firms. Below we give examples across organizational contexts.

RPA enabling digital transformation strategies. 'Digital transformation' is the most pressing C-suite concern of late. Digital transformation can enable end-to-end processes where customers search, order, receive, pay, use, operate, and maintain products and services seamlessly—a digital assembly line if you will. Getting there requires the full force of the C-suite (action principle 2) and a digital visionary that understands the customer journey.

Ian Weir, Head of Business Performance Improvement for Standard Bank of South Africa, is one such digital visionary.[21] His organization provides consulting and infuses innovations across the bank's retail, commercial, and investment business lines. For over 14 years, his group had deployed Six Sigma process improvement and operational excellence programs to improve processes, but processes were still people-centric, requiring customers and bank employees to do quite a bit of work to complete a process. Weir envisioned a world where customers would request a service on a mobile app and the service would be available within minutes. Given the banks disparate legacy systems and regulations for documentation and verification, he was not easily going to transform the bank into a digital business. He began in 2016 with the digitisation of one process, the process to apply for a current account and overdraft. In the legacy world, the process required the customer to produce pay slips, three months of bank statements, identification such as a passport, and utility bills to confirm their income, identity, and residency. The Optical Character Recognition (OCR) technology often had difficulty interpreting poor quality images, resulting in more conversations with the customer. Bank employees in call centers worked with the customer to gather all the required data, to verify the documents, and to gather additional data such as calling employers for verification of employment. The bank employees entered all the data into the bank's legacy systems to calculate credit risks and terms. The entire process took 22 days on average.

Weir's team reimagined the entire process as a digital service, beginning with using the newly available digital data services prompted by the South African government's Know Your Customer (KYC) regulations. The regulations aimed to reduce money-laundering and other criminal banking activities, but it also had another benefit: it sparked third-party companies to build and maintain databases for verification. Using these digital services—combined with credit checks to serve as a proxy for employment—and RPA,

Weir and his team digitized the entire process. Now, a customer can request a current account or overdraft on its internet platform or at a branch office, RPA pulls the required data from the third-party databases, 19 verification checks are done, the data is loaded into the legacy systems, and RPA passes the outcome back to the customer. Assuming the customer's data is current, accurate, and complete, the entire process takes just five minutes. Weir's team had 97 more use cases in the pipeline, all driving towards realizing the digital strategy. As of February 2017, Ian Weir also discussed the deployment of chatbots at the bank:

> *"Chatbots have been successfully tested and we have achieved 80 percent STP with a customer satisfaction rating of 3.8/5. This will enable customers to request services through a chat interface. Once linked to the RPA automations the customers service requests can be fulfilled 24/7 and within five minutes. Our plans are to apply this to the top 10 service query types to reduce volumes into the call centers. We are building value-adding advice into these conversations with customers. For example, capturing the reason the customer ordered the statement. If the reason is to buy a car we would offer to contact them to offer them financing. This is the start of roboadvisors using RPA in banking. Voice activated service requests like Amazon Echo are a short hop away."*

RPA enabling Global Business Service (GBS) strategies. For many Global Business Services, the business strategy was frequently about creating world-class services. For a GBS, world-class performance is characterized by an empowered staff focused on customer service and business enablement. An empowered staff delivers efficient, high-quality, responsive, scalable, flexible and compliant services. Automation became one of the levers in service transformation, along with practices such as centralization, standardization, optimization and continual improvement, and relocating labor to low cost locations (see Figure 4.1). In mature Back Office/GBS organizations, many of the transformation levers had already been deployed, thus automation was seen as the next great lever.

Consider Telefónica O2's ten-year journey of back office transformation (see Lacity and Willcocks 2016 for a detailed case study).[22] It had already centralized and standardized service and begun to offshore work from the UK to India in 2004. By 2009, the headcount in India grew to 375 FTEs and headcount in the UK was reduced to 50 FTEs. Telefónica O2 was reaching the ceiling on extracting any more value from offshoring. Its next transformation lever was eliminating non-value added processes and optimizing and simplifying the processes that remained, a lever that reduced labor headcount by ten percent. Service automation was adopted as the next transformation lever in 2010. By 2015, Telefónica O2 had automated nearly 35 percent of its back office services, reduced its reliance on its Indian-based BPO provider by a few hundred people, reduced average service response time by 50 percent for some services, and reduced customer 'chase up calls' by 80 percent. Employees were not laid off but redeployed to do more interesting work.

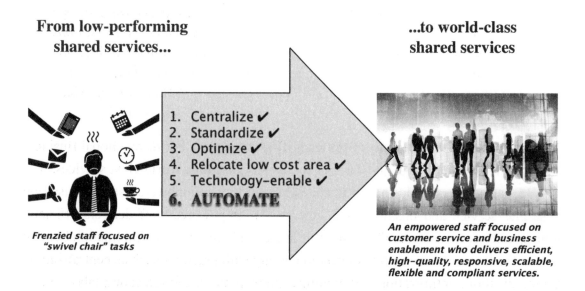

Figure 4.1: Transformation Levers for Global Business Services

Traditional BPO providers have all launched significant business strategies aimed to transform their value propositions that are largely enabled through automation. BPO providers can read the writing on the wall; as was so aptly expressed by Cliff Justice, a KPMG partner who leads the US Cognitive Automation and Digital Labor practice, when he called service automation 'the death of outsourcing'.[23]   BPO providers have to rethink how service automation will change their pricing models and service offerings, as they face questions such as: Should we create bespoke automation platforms that may lead to client technology lock-in? Or should we license a variety of independent automation solutions and bundle them with our services? Some providers struggled with cannibalizing their sales with their new RPA capabilities.

Consider the Finnish BPO provider, OpusCapita. Its clients were increasingly buying RPA projects rather than signing long-term managed contracts, undermining their revenue model. OpusCapita only took two to four weeks to complete some RPA contracts, with no contract extensions afterwards. Its RPA clients were looking for self-sufficiency and independence from external parties. In early 2016, OpusCapita was deciding how to create a successful business model in this new age of service automation (Asatiani and Penttinen 2016),[24] and this BPO provider was certainly not alone.

Advisory firms with long-standing practices in helping clients transact outsourcing agreements are pivoting significant resources to build service automation practices. In contrast to enterprise and BPO providers, advisory firms have to go broad as well as deep quickly. Credible advisors need to master a variety of tools to be 'tool agnostic' and they must understand which tools are best suited to meet a client's needs. They are building capabilities by adopting tools to automate their own internal services, by hiring RPA pioneers from early enterprise adopters, and by sending analysts through the software providers' training certification programs. As of 2016, clients understood that advisors were short-staffed on deep RPA experience; clients were looking for advisors with automation teams that could supplement rare RPA skills with other valuable expertise, such as process improvement. In 2017 the pool of RPA expertise has grown. One interviewee said in 2017, *"Now we are seeing partners who are more proactive and putting more people through RPA training. It's getting better [compared to 2016] but* *probably not running at the same speed as demand. But we have seen that if you train the right people with the right aptitude, people get up to speed very quickly."*

4.2. Cultural adoption by the C-suite

Decades of project management research identifies senior management support as a critical success factor for project success.[25] Automation programs are no different—the client organizations with C-suite support achieved the most strategic benefits from RPA. One RPA provider explained,

> *"The sites where RPA value has gone exponential is where the organization has culturally adopted automation in the C-suite, with the C-suite pushing it and driving it forward."*

According to him, divisional or IT implementations do not have sufficient breadth of influence or application: *"Here, people across the organisation look at RPA as some sort of curiosity."*

Among our cases, Xchanging's RPA adoption stands out as a good example (see Lacity and Willcocks 2015 for a detailed case study[26]). In Xchanging's 2014 Annual Report, Ken Lever, Chief Executive, wrote that Xchanging *"has invested significantly in a strategy to put technology at the heart of all our businesses."* At that time, Xchanging's corporate motto was *"technology at our core"* and its robotic process automation capability was prominently featured in its 2014 corporate annual report to shareholders.

This cultural adoption was evident in other examples. In a UK utility company, automation was embraced by the C-suite as one tool to help the company deliver service excellence to customers while minimizing price increases through lower operating costs. The Utility's CEO was the evangelist for the transformation programs, and the role technologies, including RPA, contributed to them. He spoke about RPA to C-suite executives throughout the company's regional divisions. That level of awareness and support is vital to an enterprise RPA capability.

48

4.3. Consider RPA for more than just cost savings

Cost savings are certainly an expected part of any business plan, and before looking at other business benefits, let us examine return on investment (ROI) figures from the cases more closely. As of 2016, the one-year ROIs for RPA projects ranged from a low of 30 percent to a high of 350 percent! While some people may be skeptical of triple digit ROIs, we point to the Blue Cross Blue Shield North Carolina case (see Dunlap and Lacity 2017 for the full case[27]). The automation champion presented to the CFO a one-year business case that projected a $3 million savings from a $1 million investment. The three-year business case projected savings of between $10 and $12 million dollars. When the CFO reviewed the figures, he was unconvinced, but indeed a triple digit return was generated as promised.

However savory a triple digit ROI, if clients only focus on costs they might miss opportunities for other kinds of shareholder value and, more importantly, the opportunity to improve customer experience and employee satisfaction. Clients need to consider other sources of value discussed in Chapter 2. We have found that once organizations are made aware of the triple-win, they re-conceptualize RPA as an enabler of multiple sources of value, and then re-prioritize RPA projects accordingly.

4.4. Decide who is best to 'own' the automation program

In 2015 when we began our research, organizational adoption of RPA often started bottom-up in a particular line of business operations. The business operations managers discovered RPA when they were solving a particularly pressing issue, such as taking on more routine work without being allowed to add more headcount. But now we see another pattern: senior managers are increasingly aware of RPA and its triple-win possibilities for shareholder, customer, and employee value. The C-suite envisions that Centers of Excellence (see action principle 24) will seed RPA capabilities across the enterprise. This top-down approach means better business strategies and more resources invested in vetting enterprise-worthy RPA tools, engaging helpful advisors, and training more in-house staff. Current BPO providers will increasingly compete against RPA insourcing; they will have to convince customers that their combined automation-labor models will produce value to customers over and above what they can do on their own.

As of early 2017, even with a top-down approach with full C-suite support, project ownership was typically delegated to business operations or to IT. Among the client adoption stories featured in our work, the Associated Press, Telefónica O2, Virgin Trains, Xchanging and a UK utility launched service automation in business operations. In our research, business operations typically 'owned' a service automation program when the software was designed for SMEs and when it was non-invasive IT (i.e. interfacing with presentation layers of existing systems), which includes the categories of Enterprise RPA and Desktop RPA tools (see Figure 1.2). One interviewee said, "*At the end of the day, you're onboarding a digital workforce and that workforce doesn't work for IT, so why should they report to IT?*" Even when RPA is owned by the business, IT has an important role to play (see action principles 9, 12, and 23). Since we are studying the automation of business processes (not the automation of IT processes), it makes sense that business operations lead service automation. Paul Donaldson, the RPA Lead for Xchanging at the time, reinforced the message:

> "*It's in the innovation/business part very deliberately. I'm quite protective that it shouldn't sit in the technology arm. My concern would be if you made it a technology project, you would over-engineer the process and you would end up delivering very little.*"

The empirical studies of small-scale and major IT-enabled business projects, and of IT innovation for business value, also support this finding over many years across industries and types of technology.[28] The case was summarized by Adrian Guttridge, Executive Director, Xchanging Insurance at the time, "*The technologists will back it up and provide support but it's got to be business driven, otherwise it would be perceived as being done to, not by, the business.*"

In our research, IT typically 'owned' a service automation program when the software was designed for IT professionals and when it was invasive IT (i.e. interfacing at data and business logic layers), including software development toolkits (SDK), business process management (BPM) solutions, and some RPA that require IT programming skills. IT-owned automation programs often deal with significant IT investments, like adding software capabilities to existing ERP or CRM systems of record. IT ownership is best when the objective is the efficient use of existing technical know-how; the problem is a technical one; the problem definition and the solution and implementation are clear.

In summary, we identified four action principles that give RPA its strategic intent, and dimensions. But strategy is never enough. One can throw away well-formulated, economically and organizationally feasible strategy at any stage in the long journey to RPA implementation and institutionalization. The first possible choke points are sourcing selection and tool selection. Getting off to a bad start on these will see escalating commitment to a wrong course: a commitment that becomes increasingly costly to wind back from.

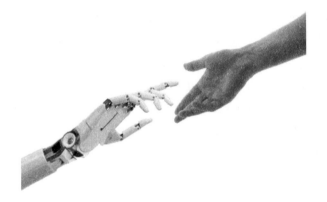

Chapter 5

Sourcing and Tool Selection Action Principles

"Risk is just an expensive substitute for information."
Adrian Slywotzky and Karl Weber

Insufficient knowledge about the advantages and disadvantages of various sourcing options and about the capabilities of different types of RPA tools, can turn out to be an expensive form of learning. In this chapter we will look at the relevant selection processes, and the action principles relevant to mitigating selection risks.

5.1. Sourcing Selection

Clients risk leaving value on the table by choosing the wrong sourcing model. Perhaps as a peculiarity of our research sample, the client organizations in our study all adopted service automation themselves, usually with the help of the service automation tool provider. But based on the survey data (and our prior outsourcing research), we think it important for other organizations considering RPA and other service automation technologies to draw on a fuller spectrum of sourcing options:

Insourcing: Here, organizations buy service automation software licenses directly from a service automation provider. The benefits of insourcing for client organizations in our study were that they had high levels of control and kept all cost savings, but this model works well only when clients have invested in building internal RPA skills for this 'do-it-yourself' (DIY) model.

Insourcing and consulting: Organizations that lack RPA capabilities may engage consulting firms to guide the service automation journey. To us, advisors are best engaged early to help clients pick the right tools. Several companies we know of delayed engaging an advisor until after they bought licenses directly from a service automation provider. While this reduced the consulting bill, some companies learned in hindsight that they bought the wrong tool for their needs.

Sourcing with a traditional Business Process Outsourcing (BPO) provider: Organizations can buy service automation as part of an integrated service delivered by a traditional BPO provider. Many traditional BPO providers have developed significant automation capabilities. The benefits of engaging a traditional BPO provider include a full suite of integrated services that combine labor arbitrage, process excellence, change management maturity and technology expertise. The risks that need to be mitigated include giving away too many of the automation benefits to the BPO provider—action principle 6 can help mitigate this risk—or getting locked in to the provider. Current pricing models in the contract, such as using FTE rate cards, can impede cooperation.

Sourcing with a pure-play: Organizations can buy service automation from a new outsourcing provider that specializes in service automation (e.g. Symphony and GenFour). One interviewee said,

> *"A pure-play firm specifically designed for RPA, that recruits, trains, retains, and builds all of its internal processes and methodologies for RPA, is going to be better at what it does than a generalist."*

Cloudsourcing: Many pundits assert that the real possibility of exploiting value lies with robotic cloudsourcing. If it take months to train a software robot to master a complex task, it takes seconds to transform the learning to another software robot located anywhere in the cloud. The major risk here is compliance, as many countries have rules about data privacy and also where customer data can be stored.

Our research uncovered two action principles related to sourcing RPA:

5.1.1 Use credible advisory firms to bridge gaps in client knowledge

By 2016, some advisory firms like Alsbridge (now ISG), Everest Group, Forrester, HfS, E&Y, and KPMG to name a few, had maturing service automation practices. During 2017, with a rising number of engagements, advisory firms are gaining the depth and breadth of knowledge that clients value. Several advisory firms created service automation landscapes to assist clients (see Figure 5.1). (Please note Figure 5.1 presents snapshots of landscapes. Tools evolve and move across the landscape over time, please contact the advisory firms for recent maps.)

In addition to tool selection, advisory firms can help clients develop service automation strategies, build business cases for automation projects, and/or build the solutions. One caveat: some advisory firms are growing so fast that they too are short of talent; be sure to engage experienced consultants for any initiative.

5.1.2. Incentivize BPO providers to share the benefits of automation

Some enterprises, like Telefónica O2's and the UK utility, receive many of their business services through outsourcing relationships. As early adopters of RPA back in 2010 and 2008 respectively, they were ahead of their BPO providers in building mature automation capabilities. In 2017, clients looking for new BPO providers have the leverage to demand more automation, lower prices, and more innovation. But for clients with existing BPO provider relationships the big issue remains: which party will benefit from automation? If the BPO contract is based on FTE rate cards, like so many are, BPO providers have little incentive to automate because any FTE savings generated from automation would reduce their revenues on that account. Therefore, clients need to incentivize existing BPO providers to automate. We know from our prior research published in Sloan Management Review that gainsharing at the project level is a good option.[29]

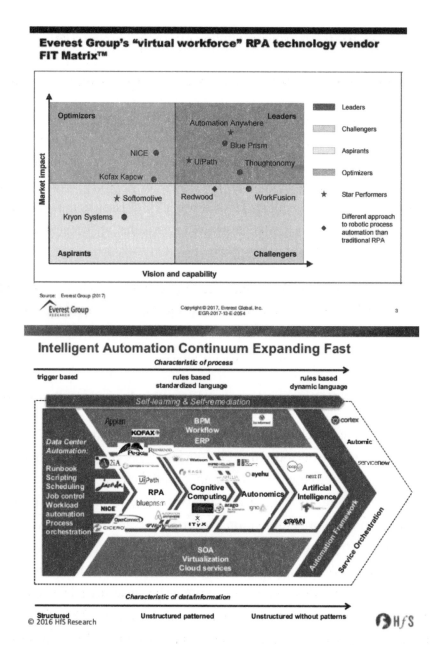

Figure 5.1: Sample of Advisory Firms' Service Automation Tool Maps
(Reprinted with permissions)

Gainsharing packs the most punch because it promises to increase the provider's revenue as well as decrease the client's invoice. ***Gainsharing was most effective when used at the project level.***[30] Clients and providers who built a business case for each innovation project, and agreed in advance how the financial compensation would be allocated, reported great results with gainsharing. In one realistic scenario based on our case study of Microsoft, the partners could share the benefits as follows. Assume an automation project reduces the number of FTEs on an account from 100 people to 90 people. Assume the provider earns revenues of $1,000,000 of which $100,000 is profits for those ten FTEs over a set time period. The client could incentivize the provider by paying twice the profits ($200,000) with the client saving $800,000. Without such a gainshare, the provider would lose revenues and profits on 10 FTEs so it would not be incented to do so.

Another scenario is that the provider changes its prices and charges the client two rate cards—one for a human FTE and one for a robotic FTE. The robotic FTE rate would be substantially lower, say 40 to 50 percent of the human rate card, but there would still be enough profit from the robots to satisfy the provider. A robotic FTE rate card, in our opinion, is likely to be the incremental step from contracts based on FTEs. A better solution will likely be to price services based on units (like price per invoice processed) or outcomes. If companies truly move to As-a-service model as evangelized by HfS[31], pricing will be based on a per service basis in the future.

5.2. Tools Selection

To mitigate the risks of choosing the wrong tool(s), too many tools, or bad tool(s), clients can pick the tool that best supports the RPA strategy, select tools based on value not just software license fees, make sure the tool is IT-safe, test multiple tools, and pick tool providers with sound financials and satisfied customers. The previous action principle of engaging an advisory firm (action principle 5) can help minimize the risks of picking a bad tool. The following action principles have helped organizations:

5.2.1. Match tool capabilities with strategic objectives

While this action principle may seem obvious, we have heard novice clients say, "I *am afraid to adopt RPA today because my organization will want the sexier artificial intelligence tools tomorrow.*" This is exactly how NOT to select a tool. RPA and CA tools are designed to automate or augment different types of tasks (see Figure 1.1)—they are complements, not substitutes. In addition to understanding which realm of tools fits a service, clients need to consider what they are trying to achieve with service automation when selecting tools. If the strategy is to democratize the workforce, then a desktop RPA solution may be the best fit for that objective. If the strategy is to '**take the robot out of the human**' in the context of rules-based enterprise transactions, then an enterprise RPA tool may be the best option. If the strategy is to augment highly skilled professionals like medical diagnosticians and financial advisors, then a cognitive tool that deals with unstructured data and inference-based processes may be optimal.

5.2.2. Consider overall value of tool capabilities, not just price

As noted in the strategy chapter, clients adopt service automation to reduce costs, but clients should not select a tool based solely on price. In practice, although all are called RPA, 'RPA' tools are by no means all the same. For example some do not scale quickly and easily. Some cannot be multi-skilled. Some are user-friendly interfaces and their software has to be fully developed by IT specialists. Clients should assess a tool on its potential value and fit. While desktop RPA is often the cheapest option, it should not be selected because of its price, it should be selected—as we just noted—based on its ability to achieve the strategic objective like democratizing the workforce. Similarly, cognitive automation tools should not be dismissed based on price because they may generate more than enough value to justify the cost.

The most savvy clients we interviewed selected tools based on price, match with strategic objectives, fit with service characteristics, and compliance with IT's infrastructure, security, and change management requirements. This is why clients need to engage their IT departments in the tool selection process, leading to the next action principle:

5.2.3. Have IT help vet the software

While business operations is best suited to evaluate an RPA product in terms of ease-of-use and fit for business purpose, RPA is still software that needs IT professionals to validate the software is enterprise worthy. As one software provider executive put it:

> *"The minute we engage with business owners, we insist on speaking with the IT function. When we talk to IT, we explain that we have a product that is designed to appease their requirements for security, scalability, auditability, and change management."*

IT can also help avoid shadow IT and the proliferations of RPA islands. Lack of centralized oversight created RPA islands in some global firms. In one financial services firm, different business units had negotiated radically different prices with the same RPA provider! If IT (or another centralized group) had aggregated demand, the company would have gotten a better deal. We also see business units selecting different tools with essentially the same functionality.[32]

5.2.4. Test tool capabilities with a controlled contest

In our case study of Telefónica O2 published in MISQ Executive[33], we noted that O2 did what most companies do when they are considering the adoption of a new technology: they did a proof-of-concept of RPA. This involved small-scale pilot trials that aimed to test the technical viability and financial value of the RPA product. An interesting twist extended the proof-of-concept into a controlled experiment when O2's IT department claimed that its BPM software could to everything the RPA software could do. This experiment allowed O2 to directly compare RPA with BPM solutions. Functionally, the solutions were nearly identical, but RPA delivered better financial value for the types of 'swivel chair' processes O2 aimed to automate. As noted in our paper, BPM software would likely have been the victor if the automation required recoding business logic or data access layers.

Some companies we studied (including O2 initially) asked their outsourcing service providers to implement RPA on their behalf. In prior research, we also found that a controlled experiment is a good way to assess provider capabilities.[34] Giving two RPA service providers the same process to automate in a controlled experiment is an excellent way to compare their capabilities. This action principle costs more upfront, but could save money on the back end.

5.2.5. Select a software provider with sound financial position and stable customers

Clients need to consider the longevity of the software provider to avoid the risk of getting stuck with a software tool that is no longer supported. By 2017 RPA had become a somewhat frenzied market because of dramatic sales growth, and this has attracted quite a lot of speculation in the market. Some RPA and CA software providers are immature, have unproven track records, negative cash flows, and uncertain futures. Some software providers have invested millions in infrastructure and only collect revenues from licensing fees. Will they remain viable? The advice is simply this: make sure the software provider has sound finances and has a proven track record of retaining clients.

In summary, we identified six further action principles that can work to mitigate risks emerging during the selection processes for sourcing and tools. Unfortunately, though, risks do not stop there. As yet RPA has not been deployed and has not seriously impacted on any interested parties. As found with other, earlier technology deployments, RPA creates new risks when it begins to be introduced into an organization. Stakeholders will also be doing their own risk analyses about how RPA is going to affect them. Stakeholder buy-in becomes an addressable area of risk.

Chapter 6

Stakeholder Buy-In Action Principles

"If you want to know how an organization works, try changing it"

Kurt Lewin

RPA initiatives require stakeholder buy-in from IT, employees, and customers, both internal and external. Each has an important role to play in realizing the value of RPA. If RPA is owned by business operations, it is vital they involve IT from the start as IT has a number of important roles to fulfill. Organizations need to take the fear away from employees by promising not to layoff people as a consequence of RPA; headcount can be ratcheted down in ways besides layoffs. Organizations need to replace employee fear with employee excitement by envisioning and delivering value to employees in terms of more interesting work, new opportunities, and recognition.

6.1. Involve IT from the start

Several early adopters, for example Telefónica O2, adopted service automation without initially involving IT. Some clients in our study said they excluded IT at the onset for two reasons: **(1)** service automation was seen as a business operations program since it required process and subject matter expertise, not IT programming skills, and **(2)** fears that IT would beleaguer the adoption with bureaucracy. In most such instances, hindsight indicated that this was a poor approach; clients learned the importance of involving the IT department from the beginning. The lesson to be learned is, 'Bring IT onboard early'. The very first step is educating the CIO, IT architecture and IT infrastructure managers about RPA. In general, IT professionals were about 6-9 months behind business operations in understanding what RPA is, how it differs from IT-led service automation tools—like software development toolkits (SDKs) and business process management solutions (BPMs)—and how RPA can be used for business advantage. Once IT understands what RPA is, IT can help validate the software as enterprise worthy, onboard the software to the IT infrastructure, and tweak access, security and change management policies to accommodate software robots.

Infrastructure management. IT is in the best position to build a scalable, safe, and robust infrastructure. IT can ensure business continuity, data and system security, and change management compliance. IT can also minimize network latency, and certainly the two early adopters that initially bypassed IT suffered latency problems. At Telefónica O2, it took about 16 weeks to optimize the infrastructure. At a UK utility company, the team initially loaded the RPA software on its existing servers; however, the RPA 'infrastructure' comprised servers with different power, memory, and operating systems which caused disparate performance and complicated management oversight. But once RPA was elevated to a strategic level, a uniform infrastructure was built. The payoff across our cases was scalability. As one senior executive put it,

> *"I know the infrastructure can scale up and down. If our processes tripled next week in size, we could probably fulfill that delivery for the processes that have been automated."*

Access management for software robots. Since several top RPA software products require a logon ID and password, IT must create access rules for robots and each robot will need its own unique identity. However, a robot's access rules will need to be different from a human's access rules. Many human accounts require unique identifiers such as employee ID numbers, national IDs such as a National Insurance Number in the UK or a Social Security Number in the US, or passport numbers. Human accounts may also require gender, age, a physical address or other fields that are not pertinent to a software robot. Password control is another issue: Who sets the robot's password? How frequently should it be changed?

In the absence of rules for a robot's access management, business operations staff worked around the rules to give robots software access. In one client organization, the RPA champion gave all the robots his ID and password, which triggered alerts in the IT security and fraud detection system. The security team quickly detained the RPA champion and he was nearly fired for violating security rules. In another company, the business operations staff made up all the data required to give the robots an account, like age, gender, and contact number. In yet another company, the RPA team came to work one day to discover the robots had stopped working—the staff forgot the IT requirement to change passwords every six months, so the accounts were suspended.

Security management for software robots. Security rules might need to be altered for software robots. For example, most organizations have security features that automatically logoff users or lock screens when the user is idle for a period of time. This security feature is an important practice for mitigating risks from human behavior, like walking away from a device without logging off the system. Furthermore, humans access software on their workstations or mobile devices that might be physically visible or accessible to non-authorized people. Software robots that are run on secured servers, on the other hand, do not share these behavioral risks. Software robots most often remain idle while waiting for another process to finish, so logging the robots off or locking their screens for idleness merely breaks the process.

IT change management for software robots. IT departments with good change management capabilities fully test any changes to software before deploying new functionality into operations. Companies that follow ITIL standards will make sure every IT change request has a unique ID, a change owner, a change priority, a description of the change, a list of the parties affected by the change, a catalog of the IT infrastructure components involved, estimates for the resources needed, a proposed schedule, an identification of risks and risk mitigation actions to be taken, and approvals. Once approved, IT will check the change thoroughly by conducting unit, string, and system interface tests. Is the same type of change management needed for RPA? Many interviewees from business operations for this research said that changing a software robot's rules is more akin to retraining a human to accommodate a new business rule. Thus, from their perspective, this level of IT oversight was not needed and merely slowed down the business. One interviewee said, *"IT organizations tell you they are agile, but peel back the covers and they're using waterfall with rafts of red-tape and change control."* He argued these changes should be in the hands of business operations, not IT, *"RPA is an operational solution and changes should be treated like operational changes"*. A better process is quality assurance of business outputs, he argued.

6.2. Communicate the value of automation to employees

As with any automation technology, some employees will feel threatened by RPA. At O2, there was fear initially among the back office and IT staff. According to Allen Surtees, an O2 Senior IT project manager at the time, *"People start fearing that this technology is going to take my job away. It's not only the people in operations; the software developers also think it's going to take their jobs away."* At O2, fears were assuaged because RPA was used to reduce FTEs in the outsourced relationship; no internal jobs were directly threatened.

If companies aim to follow our best cases, service automation will be used to get the triple win, and the 'win' for employees needs to be communicated early and frequently (see Figure 6.1).

Messaging should focus on value to employees:

- Employees will perform fewer repetitive and boring tasks
- Employees will focus more on customer service, problem solving, and complex tasks
- Employees will learn new skills (one company said millennials loved learning about software robots because they thought it was 'cool')
- Employees will gain a robot as junior co-worker
- Employees who embrace service automation will be recognized as an innovator

Xchanging took a very open approach to internal communications, making RPA visible across insurance operations, creating newsletters, and road shows. Xchanging also made sure the operations teams were engaged to support the project and understood what it meant for them six to twelve months down the line, in terms of opportunities.

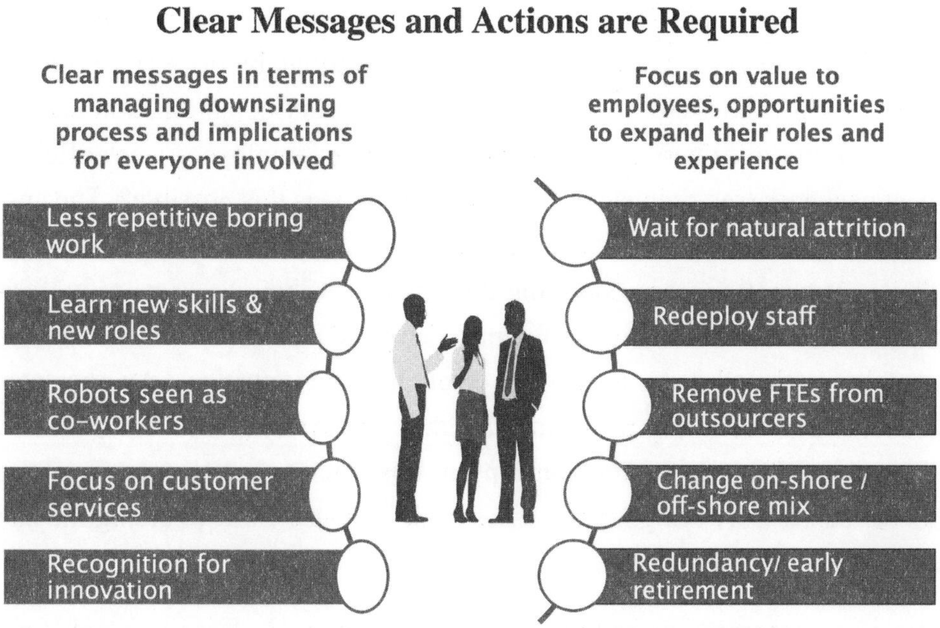

Clear Messages and Actions are Required

Figure 6.1: Practices to obtain employee buy-in

6.3. Promise no layoffs as a consequence of service automation

One reason why companies need to promise employees no layoffs as a consequence of service automation is that it is difficult to get employees to build their own guillotines. But a bigger reason is that if companies are using automation strategically, employees should benefit from automation. Across our case studies, we have seen clients use service automation tools to automate very repetitive and boring work, freeing up internal staff to work on tasks that are more varied, complex, and interesting. Staff members from many of our cases were not threatened by automation, but rather welcomed the benefits of performing fewer repetitive tasks and more customer-facing roles. At one early adopter, RPA has been around for so long that it is not perceived as a threat. One senior executive told us, *"People see automation as an opportunity to improve what they do."* For companies in growth mode, automation helped avoid hiring more people, enabling the organization to take on more work without more people.

What happens when automation scales to the point when fewer people are needed? So far, we have not seen internal layoffs directly attributable to service automation; the internal staffs who were no longer needed after service automation scaled were redeployed to other business activities, or in one case, employees were offered early retirement packages (see right side of Figure 6.1). How is this possible? The answer is that all these organizations were experiencing dramatic increases in the amount of work to be done. Automation was addressing the problem of how to do more with similar, or slightly less, human resources, differently deployed. To achieve this, one company incrementally ratcheted down headcount through natural attrition. Another company slowed down their recruiting program. We did, however, see two companies reduce FTEs from their BPO provider relationships, as this practice was seen as a way to regain control over services by bringing processes back in-house while avoiding the backlash of internal employee layoffs.

But what if an organization intends to layoff employees? Prior research finds that communicating the intended effect on jobs early in the process is by far the best practice.[35] In a communications vacuum, employees overestimated jobs losses. In many cases, staff members panicked and some even sabotaged new initiatives. Many organizations find it difficult to retain the cooperation of employees targeted for redundancy. In one case study of Reuters that we published in *MISQ Executive*[36], Reuters was very careful to treat fairly employees who would be made redundant and found a way to ensure they were accountable for the success of the migration of work. Although the context of this case was offshoring work, the lessons may apply to automation as well. First, Reuters gave employees plenty of notice. Some people who were to be let go were given 18 months advance notice that they would no longer have a job at Reuters. Second, Reuters built into the retention package a requirement that employees facilitate and sign off on the transfer of their work.

6.4. Select 'rising-stars' for service automation projects

In addition to picking the right services for RPA (covered in the next chapter), managers also need to pick employees who throw themselves into the automation projects. These folks are often 'rising stars', employees who seek new challenges, become obsessed at execution, but get easily bored. Organizations should target 'rising stars' for both management and technical assignments. The 'rising star' *managers* on launch projects might become heads of the automation CoE when the organization matures. Organizations need to offer these stars rich career opportunities and attractive compensation or other companies will poach them. Indeed, many of the RPA rising stars we interviewed in 2015 had moved to new companies in positions of leadership by 2017.

The 'rising star' technicians are typically not looking for managerial responsibilities but rather a succession of new technologies to master. For Ascension Health, millennials with a gaming background proved to be good employees to staff on RPA projects because they enthusiastically discovered how to use the new tools and enjoyed putting in concentrated amounts of time to get automations to work. Such 'rising stars' are great to get new tools functioning, but they will get bored if assigned to ongoing RPA maintenance.

6.5. Redesign employee scorecards

Across our automation case studies, RPA took over the dreary tasks to allow employees to focus on more value-added work. One consequence is that an individual's productivity will decline after automation because the humans now deal with more complex work as the robots take over the easy tasks. For example, in one case study that automated healthcare claims, the average human productivity metric was about 12 claims per hour before automation. After automation, human productivity fell to about seven claims per hour because the claims examiners were dealing with only difficult claims. Obviously, the assessment of human productivity had to be redesigned after automation. Rather than focusing on 'productivity' in terms of claims processed by a human examiner per hour, the healthcare company needed to apply metrics to *gauge the effectiveness of combined human-automation team*. The balance had to be right. If, for example, the RPA sent an exception to a human that the human could quickly resolve, then that situation very likely indicated an opportunity for further automation.[37] Other case companies avoided the productivity measure altogether by assessing employee performance based on customer satisfaction or service quality.

In summary, in this chapter we have provided five further action principles, here addressing the risk of lack of stakeholder buy-in. The time has come to launch the RPA project. As we saw in the Foreword (see Figure A3), IT-based business projects engender some typical generic content and process risks. In the next chapter, we use the evidence from our RPA-specific research to add to this picture

Chapter 7

Launch/Project Action Principles

"A risk is a potential for a loss. The loss is the realization of that negative potential. A risk is running across a busy street blindfolded. A loss is getting hit by a car while doing that." **Riskviews**

"There are only six things that can go wrong with a project. The problem is that it's a different six each time." **Senior manager, Financial Services**

Organizations have several risks to mitigate during RPA launch to prevent initial projects from failing technically, financially, and/or politically. Picking the right projects to automate is paramount.

7.1 Select 'wow' projects based on impact to customers and employees

Here is the common wisdom on selecting services for automation. *RPA experts and early adopters report that RPA is most suitable for processes with high transaction volumes, high levels of standardization, and that are highly rules-based, mature and stable.*[38] The thinking goes as follows: High transaction volumes provide the most opportunity for reducing costs.[39] The easiest processes to automate with RPA have high degrees of process standardization so that the process is always performed consistently and that all of the company's business units expect the same service.[40] Processes that are highly rules-based are also easier to automate because RPA software needs explicit instructions.[41] Mature processes are easier to automate because they are measured, well-documented, and predictable, and their costs are known.[42] Stable processes mean that the robots will need less re-configuring. For Xchanging, stability was a major criterion:

> *"Don't automate a process that's not ready to be automated. Stabilize it first. It's a basic Six Sigma principle.... In all of our processes, we keep a delivery lead in the process world, to standardize and streamline before we automate."*
> **Paul Donaldson, then Group Project Manager for Robotic Automation, Xchanging**

In addition to these criteria, RPA can deal effectively with complex processes as long as complexity is defined as requiring compound steps and the control of many variables. One advantage of 'Enterprise' RPA (see Figure 1.2) is that it is highly interoperable and can readily run on any platform—mainframes, client/server, or cloud systems. Early adopters have also reported that compliance risks are minimal with RPA because every action executed by RPA software is logged and thus auditable.[43]

Organizations will find many processes that meet the task characteristics just discussed. So which automation projects should rise to the top of the priority list? ***Companies that achieved the fastest uptake and the most value from RPA, selected projects based on impact to customers and employees in addition to contribution to shareholder value.*** They also prioritized projects that addressed visible, felt pain-points in the process or organization. These projects touched customers and liberated their employees. Consider the Associated Press. Lou Ferrara, head of business and sports news at the time, decided to automate corporate earnings reports. Corporate earnings reports had significant volume—journalists wrote about 300 of them each quarter. The investment data used to write the reports were highly structured, standardized, and stable. The reports had a standard template. Overall, journalists hated this boring assignment. The automation delivered multiple benefits—the AP went from covering 300 companies to over 4,000 companies each quarter, bringing more news to more customers. The reports were generated faster, and had fewer errors. The journalists were freed up to work on more exciting assignments. The AP did generate modest savings of three FTEs, but by picking this visible project to launch rather than one that had the largest

FTE savings, the AP got the company and the outside world excited about automation. The uniqueness of the context gained Ferrara media attention and global speaking engagements, including in China.[44] The AP went on to add new services via automation, like covering college sports, as they scaled adoption. However, exciting applications still need a solid business case, as discussed next.

7.2. Build realistic business cases

Companies just beginning their RPA journeys frequently had unrealistic expectations about what RPA can deliver, how fast it can deliver, and what benefits will result. Unrealistic business cases can sour an organization on RPA and certainly result in little value. Good business cases consider the following in their estimates of costs and benefits:

How clean is the data? RPA can automate tasks that follow rules to process structured data. This means that the organization must have clean data (structured, complete, and accurate). In reality, many organizations have dirty data that will need human intervention to fix. Increasingly, cognitive automation is being targeted to transform unstructured data into structured data for RPA processing, but that does not solve the issues of data incompleteness or data inaccuracy.

Are business rules standard and agreed-upon? Ludwig von Bertalanffy, the father of General Systems Theory[45], used the term 'equifinality' to describe the phenomenon that a given end can be reached by many means in biological and social systems. We see this phenomenon in much of human work; humans often enact different ways to accomplish tasks successfully, even though all of the ways comply with the rules. For RPA, *one way* needs to be designed. Is that *one* right way agreed upon?

Are business rules documented? If documentation is incomplete or outdated, the business case needs to include time to document the 'as-is' process in the business case. Furthermore, most businesses typically only document the optimal path—or the 'happy path' as one interviewee described it—and not the myriad of exceptions.

Realistically, businesses should expect RPA to first automate the most common path and then add rules to accommodate less common paths over time (see action principles 20 and 28).

Are the business rules detailed enough for instructing a robot? Humans are proficient at following general rules like, 'get your supervisor to sign the expense report.' A software robot cannot execute rules at this level. The software robot would need details like: :

'Logon to HR system' with precise details on how to fill in the logon screen
'Find employee record' with precise details on how to search
'Search for supervisor name' (more details…)
'Extract email address' (more details…)
'Logoff HR system' (more details…)
'Logon to email system' (more details…)
'Paste email address' (more details…);
'Append the expense report' (more details…)
'Add the text
'Attached please find an expense report for your approval.'

One gets the idea. **Business cases need to include the time to transform human rules into robot rules** (see action principle 19). One caveat here: Record buttons on some RPA products will speed this process initially, but any changes later on will result in the entire process being re-recorded.

Will the business commit to the results? In some organizations, business cases included FTE reduction as the main benefit to shareholders. After RPA was deployed, senior managers demanded to know, *"Why do you still have the same number of people?"* As explained above, RPA has much more value to offer than just FTE savings. We suggested that if FTE reduction is an aim, it is best to wait for natural attrition or to slow recruiting rather than lay off employees. **We also think 'hours saved back to the business' is a better promise to make in a business case.** One healthcare provider reported giving 49,951 hours back to the business in 2016. What might an organization do with those extra hours?

7.3. Redesign human work for robotic work

Although some companies chose to automate the 'as-is' process to speed implementation, companies that took the time to redesign processes for robotic automation had much better experiences in terms of long-term operations. One common issue is that a human tends to perform swivel chair processes throughout the day by logging on and off the same systems many times. For RPA, a better design batches work for the software robots by configuring them to logon once and to execute all the transactions associated with that process for the day (or week or month).

Another consideration is number of handoffs between humans and the software robots. If a human has to intervene at too many points, end-to-end processing time may not be significantly reduced. Royal DSM, a Dutch multinational company, redesigned its processes for RPA. The company removed some tasks within a process and completed them at another time. For example, intercompany reconciliations could be done all the time with robotics rather than just during month end close when the humans used to do them. Royal DSM also discovered that some steps could be eliminated altogether—they were just legacy tasks because 'we've always done it this way.' An example was asset depreciation, where the robot ran the process in test mode and if there were no errors, automatically proceeded to a production run. (See full case study by Lacity and Willcocks 2016[46]). Figure 7.1 displays the challenge of optimizing the sequence of steps using a hypothetical scenario.

7.4 Consider Pareto's Principle

Back in 1896, the Italian economist, Vilfredo Pareto, observed that 80 percent of the land in Italy was owned by 20 percent of the people. Pareto claimed this distribution was evident in all sorts of natural and social phenomenon. In nature, 20 percent of peapods produced 80 percent of peas (at least in Pareto's garden). Since that time, the distribution has been frequently observed. In business, the rule posits that 80 percent of results (e.g. profitability) stem from 20 percent of efforts. In software maintenance, some companies have observed that fixing 20 percent of software bugs fixed 80 percent of reported errors. In software design, it is argued that 80 percent of the work will be accomplished in 20 percent of the time and 20 percent of the work will take 80 percent of the time. For RPA, the rule would posit that automating only 20 percent of the possible paths in a process will handle up to 80 percent of the transactions. In short, **automate the most common paths in a process first—rare exceptions and uncommon routes within a process are costly to automate.** This captures most of the value rapidly and any mistakes can be quickly fixed.

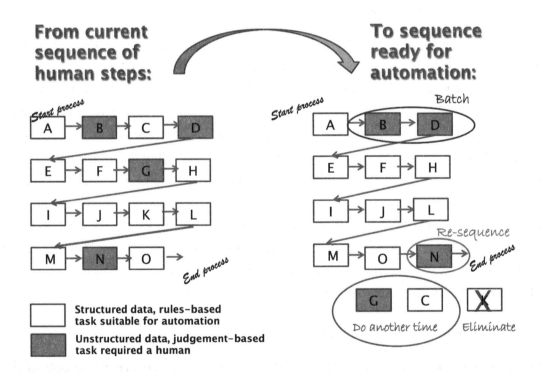

Figure 7.1: Optimizing the Sequence of Steps in an End-to-End Process

NOTE - The left hand side of the figure depicts an end-to-end process with 15 steps currently being done by a human. Some of those steps, those in clear boxes, entail structured data and rules-based processes, such as looking up data fields in an existing system of record. Some tasks, depicted with yellow boxes, require judgment, interpretation, or problem-

solving skills. When examining this process for automation, only the clear boxes are suitable for RPA, but the current sequencing would require the human to intervene four times. To optimize the sequence for automation, an RPA team might realize that some tasks are not needed and can be eliminated (like task K depicted on the right hand side), some tasks can be pulled out of the process and done at another time (like tasks G and C), and some tasks that require human intervention might be batched (like B and D) or re-sequenced (like N).

A 'time-box' approach will help prevent scope creep. 'Time-boxing' gave a short deadline, e.g. three months for a live business deliverable—in Xchanging's case, for example, for the first four processes. If this is not feasible, break the project down into a series of smaller projects, each with a business deliverable. Our recommendation on IT-enabled business projects has been to go for 'dolphins not whales', i.e. small projects based on iterative learning, with quick business payoffs, though the technology used must be consistent with the IT architecture and infrastructure of the organization. Large 'whale' projects tend to go over budget, experience time delays, and sub-optimize on delivery.[47] Once the common routes are delivered and stable, organizations can then continually improve them and automate more paths (see action principle 28).

In summary, we highlighted four further Action Principles won from the hard learning ground of client RPA launch and project experiences. In the next chapter, focusing on operations and change management, we discover further distinctive RPA risks, and how these can be mitigated.

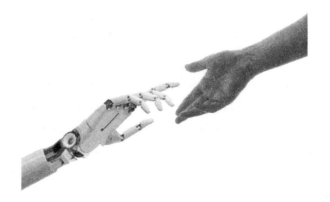

Chapter 8

Operations/Change Management Action Principles

"He who rejects change is the architect of decay."

Harold Wilson

Organizations need to mitigate a number of operational and change management risks to ensure the robotic workforce operates efficiently, adapts to changes, and performs well over time. Sound operations and change management begin with the realization that software robots are different than other types of software: **A software robot should be considered a hybrid—half worker, half software.** Software robots are part of the workforce, so they need to be managed like humans. They are also IT products that need to be managed like software. This hybrid creature requires a different kind of management that many organizations have not yet encountered. Several action principles assure that the software robots are work-ready, and that changes to them are coordinated and managed to keep them robust, responsive, and efficient.

8.1. Make sure the robots are work-ready

When organizations only view software robots as IT software, they may apply traditional IT testing procedures to ascertain when the software robots are ready to be moved into production. Traditional IT tests might include unit, system, and integration tests to verify the software robots can be launched, and that robots can be started and stopped, for example. In most organizations, development environments are subtly different than production environments. Differences are tolerable for IT products, but not for software robots. For example, if the development environment has a different logon screen than the production environment, the robots won't work in production. Testing all the data types and process steps is vital. Richard Hilditch, Chief Robotic Operating Model (ROM) Architect for Blue Prism explained, "*Automation testing is all about quality assurance. You are actually assuring that the work the robot has done is correct. You have to have confidence the robot is doing the right thing for all scenarios.*" So when are robots work ready? **Software robots are work ready when all the scenarios of the process have been verified in a development environment that is an exact copy of the production environment.**

8.2. Manage the robotic workforce

As a digital workforce, the robots need oversight. Several organizations initially treated the digital workforce as they would new employees by verifying all the robot's work at first and then gradually trusting the robot to perform with less oversight. One interviewee from a company that initially verified every key step, said, "*We can start optimizing by taking some controls out… we now trust how it works.*"

However, the human manager can never fully disappear. One interviewee said, "*Organizations need to recognize that these robots are a digital workforce. You need to treat them like a workforce and not an application. People think you can automate 100 percent of a process and be done. But the digital workforce needs to be looked after: Did they turn up for work? Did they complete the assignment? Did they encounter something new that requires our help? You still need to do performance reviews and teach them new rules when things change.*"

8.3. Assign clear boundaries of responsibility

Thus far, we have described some similarities and differences between humans and software robots. As a hybrid, software robots need an operating model that clearly defines the roles of IT and business operations. We present one such operating model that was developed by Blue Prism.

Blue Prism offers an operational model of IT and business role assignments to ensure value from RPA (see Figure 8.1). We focus on the IT roles first. David Moss, CTO for Blue Prism explained six roles for IT: enterprise infrastructure, regulatory compliance, supported platform, secured environment, scalable cloud deployment, and operational assurance:

> "**Enterprise infrastructure** *ensures the platform runs on scalable, secured, and resilient hardware that is constantly monitored and administered by experts to ensure business continuity and room for growth (e.g. in a data center not on a desktop), and that the environment is backed up, able to be restored and is run like a 'proper' enterprise technology service—e.g. it's available.* **Regulatory Compliance** *means that compliance teams ensure that roles are segregated, security is appropriate, and data is held in such a way that solutions configured on the platform conform to legislative requirements.* **A Supported Platform** *is something that is provided to the business with a service level and availability contract that can be relied on to perform their business critical processes, e.g. the opposite of what a power cut would do to something that was running unmanaged in an open office. The environment needs to be secured appropriately to ensure that access is restricted—to prevent data being compromised—and so that access cannot be gained without an audit trail or appropriate permissions, e.g. people walking past an open desktop in an office looking at what the robot is doing and seeing customer data, or taking over the process in the desktop example.* **Scalable** *cloud deployment describes how a good architecture can allow organizations to easily increase capacity when there is a peak in demand by using on demand hosting technologies.* **Operational Assurance** *combines the above to provide the operation with a level of service that complies with their customer SLA contracts, and provides a platform that can run mission critical processes with consideration for disaster recovery, failover, multiple sites processing the data in the case of site loss, and contingency planning for processes that go offline."* ***David Moss, CTO, Blue Prism.***

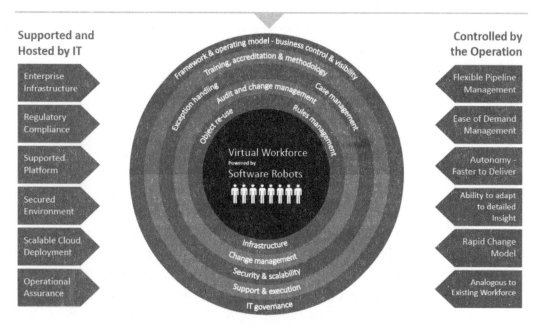

Figure 8.1: Partnership between Operations and IT
(Source: Blue Prism, reprinted with permission)

According to the Blue Prism model, operations is in charge of pipeline management, ease of demand, autonomy over delivery, ability to adapt to detailed insight, rapid change model, and control over the digital workforce. We address these operational roles in action principles 24 and 25, discussed in the next chapter.

To summarize, in this chapter we focused on how risks with RPA arise when active management of the software robots is lacking. This led to our identification of three operational and change management action principles. There is a danger when getting this far, as operations stabilize, of complacency, lack of ambition, and missed business potential. Managers need to loop back to, and make sure they are aligned with, the strategic intent and ambition established in Chapters 2 and 4. In our final chapter we put forward a further seven action principles that push the organization into building not just an RPA, but also an automation capability.

Chapter 9

Road to Maturity Action Principles

"The best way to predict your future is to create it."

Peter Drucker

When a company experiences the triple-win value from its first RPA deployments, they aim to expand RPA across the enterprise. A number of practices help organizations achieve mature capabilities, including building an RPA center of excellence (CoE), rethinking talent, multi-skilling the software robots, reusing components, continually improving existing automations, integrating tools to automate services end-to-end, and finally, integrating different automation efforts under one service automation CoE.

9.1. Establish a Center of RPA Excellence

The road to maturity can begin with the creation of an RPA CoE. The main duties of an RPA CoE are

- demand management,
- feasibility assessment,
- development of business cases for each automation project,
- project prioritization,
- automation development,
- automation implementation,
- monitoring & support, and continuous improvement.

A CoE also establishes standards and best practice, and tracks the business performance of service automation.

Among all of our cases, a UK utility company had one of the most mature RPA capabilities and thus provides a good example of an RPA CoE. The utility structured service automation governance using a federated model. The CoE was part of a large division where RPA was first adopted but had direct reports seeded in the other divisions. The CoE comprised about nine people: an RPA manager, four developers, two control room staff, a configuration coordinator, and a portfolio analyst. Small, distributed RPA teams were housed in three other business units.

The CoE at the utility managed service automation demand (number 1 in Figure 9.1). Demand for automations was high and typically came from customer transformation programs and from operational teams in the business divisions. Candidate processes were put through the pipeline where the CoE assessed their automation worthiness. The CoE, in cooperation with the requesting business operations area, developed a business case if automation looked promising. With clear instructions on how the process worked and what the transaction times were, the CoE produced a project initiation document, to be signed off by business users, automation developers, and other invested parties (see number 2 in Figure 9.1).

The CoE used RPA Developers to build the automated solutions and a Control Room team to operate the software robots once they were in production. The RPA developers were heavily involved with business stakeholders and operations team in the beginning.

The RPA developers documented the project, developed the RPA solution, tested the solution by verifying results, then handed control over to the Control Room team once the robots were live.

The Control Room team then took over full management of the live RPA process, including interacting with the business operations folk to coordinate the daily stream of work, the output reports and exceptions (see number 3 in Figure 9.1).

Besides the normal control room work, the CoE aimed to continually improve the solution (see action principle 28). The Control Room team also received change requests directly from business operations users, which it handed back to the RPA developers.

So the cycle of improvement continued (see number 4 in Figure 9.1). The CoE provides the structure and governance to build enterprise RPA capabilities, but the CoE needs to be staffed with the right talent.

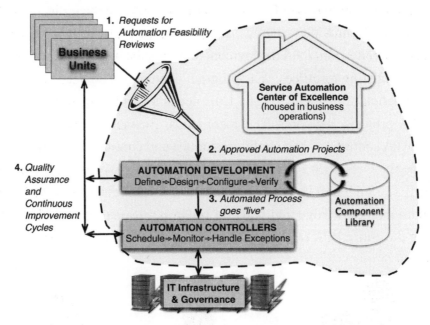

Figure 9.1: An RPA Center of Excellence

9.2. Rethink talent development for skills needed for an enterprise automation capabilities

Organizations need to rethink skillsets, roles, and job descriptions as they build mature RPA capabilities. Initially, one person typically undertook several RPA roles, but as the RPA capability matured many organizations assigned people to better-defined specialist roles. For example, A.J. Hanna at Ascension Ministry Service Center said:

> *"We have started the process of dedicating the automation team members into business requirements and documentation specialists, process modeling specialists and configuration specialists. This will allow us to increase our output by putting a specific focus on each of the stages of automation."*

A mature RPA capability has identified the various roles for managing the RPA program (see Figure 9.2). The RPA program needs a program champion to lead the CoE and he or she needs support from the C-suite (see action principle 2). A C-suite executive champion may spend only two to four percent of their time on the project, but the role is to mandate direction, provide resources, and protect the project. The business sponsor stands to gain directly from RPA deployment and must be actively engaged in winning support and mobilizing resources. The program champion also needs ongoing support from IT (see action principle 22). The CoE needs a number of roles to develop and maintain RPA projects, including RPA team leads, Business Process Architects, RPA developers, RPA controllers, and quality assurance and continuous improvement talent. From outside the CoE, each RPA project needs a business sponsor and subject matter experts (SMEs). Such users and managers from the business need to be brought in to provide additional knowledge and reaction on an occasional basis. The SMEs work closely with the entire RPA team to help define the business rules, identify test cases, and verify outcomes.

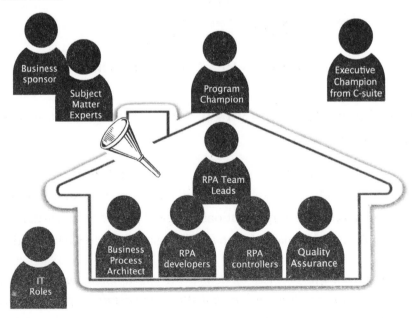

Figure 9.2: Key RPA roles

RPA Program Champion. A strong program manager is needed, someone who champions RPA, engages closely with the C-suite and business sponsors, and understands how to get a program of projects delivered within budgets and schedules. This person should have experience, personal credibility and political clout within the organization, which normally requires a senior person. One interviewee described the role as, *"His/ her job is to make sure that elements that need to be engaged from the business side are engaged."* The demand for this position is high, skills are rare, and organizations will need to compensate this person accordingly.

RPA Business Process Architects. RPA architects need to deeply understand as-is processes and how to improve the process before transforming human work for robotic work (see action principle 19). Specifically, architects need to understand how to break down a process into smaller steps, create reusable objects, and how to optimize the process sequence to get the most value from robots. RPA architects must be able to work closely with subject matter experts to get the process right, as well as with IT to make sure the solution will work on the platform. Concerning the latter, one architect designed an easy-to-use front-end for SMEs to input new rules for the robots once they were in production, but the design did not initially consider the version control required by IT. The RPA architect subsequently worked with IT for a solution that complied with change management policies. One interviewee explained, *"It's a bit like the tortoise and the hare. Spend more time architecting your design and you'll end up with a robust, efficient process that you can maintain at a much lower cost."*

RPA Developers. RPA developers build the solutions designed by RPA architects. These roles were often recruited internally and trained for the job. What skills might they need? The utility company looked to recruit RPA developers from operations staff with a strong understanding of the business, a logical mind, and preferably a systems analysis background. The overriding requirement to be on the RPA team was to be able to extract logical structures from chaotic business data so that prescribed algorithms can be built. IT skills were also valued, but one manager said, *"We're not IT staff but we have staff with IT skills."*

RPA Controllers. Controllers needed to plan the day and organize the workload vis-à-vis other system priorities, such that the correct work is sequenced and the correct number of robots are activated. The controllers also need good communication skills because they interact with business operations people when they spot any issues or anomalies. For the Control Room staff, the utility looked to recruit people who were organized, methodical, and logical, and had a consistent approach to work. Utility's Control Room team had matured to the point where two people controlled a workforce of 300 robots. At peak times, those two controllers orchestrated the work output equivalent to more than 600 people. At another company, a bank had three teams of two people that work in shifts to control nearly 400 robots.

Quality Assurance. During development, this role ensures that all the test cases identified by the SMEs work correctly in the development environment. When CoEs were short-staffed, the developer sometimes performed this role, but this violates a basic software design principle that software developers should not test their own code. Once in production, this role monitors the outputs to ensure robots continue to function properly.

9.3. Multi-skill the software robots

Multi-skilling the robots is also a practice of a mature RPA capability. For one financial service firm in our study, the fact that its robots can be multi-skilled was a real benefit. A senior executive said:

> *"A piece that I think is very attractive is the ability to use the robots on multiple tasks. From a robot, I just say, 'do the payroll run this morning and in your downtime, go over and do this task in accounting that's at a different time of day' and that, I can see, is incredibly powerful."*

In contrast to robots, the human workforce tends to be assigned to specific work units; humans typically cannot be dynamically re-assigned to balance out demand fluctuations across units. A payroll clerk in shared services typically cannot, for example, be asked

86

to perform the work of an accounting clerk to balance out workloads. An Xchanging executive told us:

> *"Multi-skilling. I'm amazed people don't do this... Get all robots on your virtual servers able to do any process. You can get them doing stuff when they've got no other work to do, and it doesn't cost you anything extra. It's an easy win that few follow."*

For enterprise RPA tools, multi-skilled robots pull tasks from component libraries for execution, as explained next.

9.4. Reuse components to scale quickly and to reduce development costs

Some RPA products are based on 'object-oriented' robots whose tasks can be stored and reused in an automation component library. Recall the example of detailing rules for robotic execution from action principle 18: RPA with a component library capability means each task only has to be defined once and can be pulled from the library on many different automations. Service automation productivity skyrockets as more reusable components are added to and taken from the library.

The development times for implementing an RPA project at a utility company were reduced by between 30 and 40 percent because of the reusable components. The utility company built a library of robotic processes, which were reused on other automation projects. With RPA, the turnaround time was much faster than for requested changes in the mainframe system. The RPA provider account manager explained further how component reuse lowered the development costs. He said:

> *"It's a self-fulfilling prophecy, the more processes you automate, the more objects you build in your robotic library, therefore, the more reuse you get, therefore, the assembly and delivery costs of those objects into new processes becomes more and more economic."*

9.5. Continually improve and expand existing automations

This action principle is the follow-up to The Pareto Principle (action principle 20). Initially, organizations are advised to automate the most common paths in a process. For example at an insurance company, RPA initially only processed 15 percent of the paths for a Payment Protection Insurance (PPI) process, with subsequent iterations capturing more and more exceptions. For processes that change frequently, like PPI rules, 80 percent automation may be the ceiling for RPA delivery. A manager from a utility company provided another example:

> *"So you're not going for the 100 percent automation, an all singing, all dancing solution. But you might go for a 30 percent first of all… an incremental approach allows you to manage your expectations and also makes sure that the foundations you're putting down in that system and for that process, are robust and secure and actually work and deliver."*

The utility had since developed a mature demand management capability to identify processes worth automating. Within an end-to-end process, the company automated a range of sub-processes from as high as 100 percent automation to as low as two percent.

9.6. Integrate tools to automate services end-to-end

In 2015, clients we studied had adopted a single tool as its first step in a service automation journey. But because tools are suited to different tasks and infrastructure environments, integrating several automation tools can create a multiplier effect. Consider one BPO we studied in charge of processing invoices for its client. The client's customers submit invoices to an email mailbox, which gets loaded into the ERP work queue. In the past, a human had to do much of the checking to match each invoice line item with a legitimate PO number and legitimate PO line item. The BPO provider now extracts all the legitimate PO numbers and line items from the invoices, then sends them to a cognitive automation provider that populates a structured template with the data, which is then passed back to the BPO provider.

Optical Character Recognition (OCR) tools, CA tools, and RPA tools are increasingly being integrated. One insurance company calls their OCR tools the 'eyes of the robot', with OCR feeding directly into the RPA tool. Traditional OCR software is getting better at converting images to text with time, but it is still not 100 percent accurate. According to Cvision, a typical OCR accuracy rate is about 98 percent on a good quality image,[48] which means that there will still be about 200 errors on a 10,000 word document (about 30 pages). OCR accuracy rates increase when the software is enhanced with a good supervised machine-learning algorithm. Advanced OCR tools (or OCR tools paired with a new CA tool) can further automate the extraction of data from images such as faxes, paper documents, and PDFs into structured digital formats. For example, if an OCR tool has already learned to find a purchase order number by extracting phrases from images like 'purchase order #', 'PO number', 'PO #', it would generate an exception check for human review when it encountered for the first time another version of the field, say for example, 'PO num'. A human would confirm this is indeed another valid extraction of the purchase order number field, and the software would not need human intervention next time it reads it. Some versions of OCR also weight its 'guess', and humans can decide, based on the accuracy needs of the context, what the threshold weight for human review should be.

9.7. Integrate automation initiatives: From RPA CoE to Automation CoE

In 2016, we began research on cognitive automation (CA) adoptions. Interestingly, several of the companies launching CA also had an RPA CoE. However, the two automation initiatives—that is CA and RPA programs—were managed by different organizational units. Whereas an RPA CoE was typically housed in business operations, the CA initiatives were typically owned by a centralized innovation or R&D group. The sizes of CA investments were significantly greater than RPA investments, and therefore required different levels of approval. Also, RPA was seen as 'today's' tool that could be quickly deployed, whereas the CA adoptions were more speculative and seen as 'tomorrow's' tool. We think that it makes sense to integrate these initiatives going forward as organizations realize that both RPA and CA realms enable business strategies; together they can complement and magnify value. In general, we foresee service **automation CoEs** that bring the full force of the service automation landscape under one centralized center. We think this center will report to a Chief Digital Strategy Officer or other C-suite executive. In early 2017, we already saw evidence of this prediction. At one financial services firm, the company had a CoE for CA and a CoE for RPA in 2016, but began to align their efforts in 2017.

The Bigger Picture: SMAC/BRAID

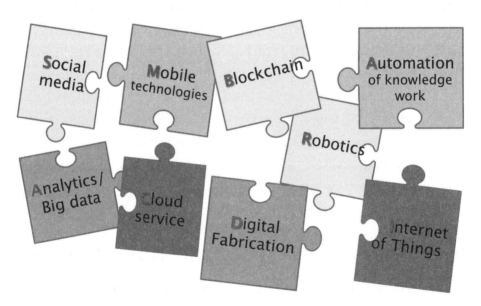

Figure 9.3: The Bigger Picture: SMAC/BRAID

Increasingly, organizations will create competitive advantage by connecting various innovations such as **S**ocial media, **M**obile technologies, **A**nalytics and Big Data, **C**loud services, **B**lockchains, **R**obotics, **A**utomation of knowledge work (like RPA and CA), the **I**nternet-of-Things, and **D**igital Fabrication (i.e. 3-D printing), which we call SMAC/BRAID (see Figure 9.3), for service delivery. Organizations usually experiment with new technologies in innovation labs, but getting vetted technologies out of digital labs and into CoEs focused on rapid delivery will become a competitive differentiator.

Chapter 10

Conclusion

"A ship is safe in harbor. But that's not what ships are for."　　**G.T. Shed**

"(You) that will not apply new remedies must expect new evils: for time is the greatest innovator."　**Francis Bacon**

In this research, we aimed to provide a definitive guide for mitigating RPA risks to help managers deliver value to shareholders, customers, and employees. The research is based on the lessons learned from real RPA implementations across a variety of industries and countries. Key to all of our work is the important notion that managers actively design the way we use tools. Too much popular rhetoric espouses a philosophy of technological determinism by positing that automation technologies will lead to massive unemployment—a view that we contest. Instead, we view managers as thoughtful agents who can design technologies to benefit many stakeholders. This is why, when we are asked, 'Does RPA and CA lead to massive layoffs?' we answer with empirical data. Our cases provide evidence of work being reconfigured and of workers being redeployed rather than made redundant. Rising workloads meant that more work was being done, while people were assigned a richer mix of tasks, as a result of service automation. Early days, perhaps?

When reviewing projections of automation on employment, we advise people to make sure they understand the underlying assumptions. The best studies analyze tasks within occupations rather than assuming an entire occupation will be automated.[49] The most valid studies also consider that new jobs will be created.[50] The more thoughtful studies discount an "automation tsunami" and point to how long technologies take to actually deploy and for their full business potential to be realized. The data explosion from SMAC/BRAID will create many new jobs to both exploit the data opportunities as well as to mitigate cybersecurity threats. People will be needed to deal with the proliferation of regulations designed to protect data in an increasingly connected world. Indeed, the US Department of Labor in 2013 asserted, *"65% of today's students will be employed in jobs that don't exist yet"*.[51] Humans will continue to provide tasks that require empathy, creativity, tacit knowing, ethical integrity, and leadership; humans will continue to imaginatively combine ideas from diverse contexts to develop new products and services; humans will remain superior at functioning better than machines in completely novel situations, to list but a few.

Our human qualities will remain vital in the future of work.

Appendix

Research Methodology

To investigate Robotic Process Automation (RPA) and Cognitive Automation (CA) we conducted two surveys and interviewed 61 people, including service automation adopters, providers, and advisors.

Surveys

We surveyed the attendees of the 2015 and 2016 Outsourcing World Summit (OWS) during the client-only and provider/advisor-only networking sessions.[52] The 2015 sample of 143 completed surveys consisted of 63 clients, 64 providers, and 16 advisors. The survey assessed the maturity of service automation adoption, the drivers of service automation adoption, the perceived automatability of existing business services, and the preferred sourcing option.

The client respondents were senior leaders in charge of sourcing strategy, governance, procurement and provider management. They are responsible for IT Infrastructure, software development, financial and accounting, human resource, logistics, call center, and/or research & development services, and outsourcing relationships within their organizations. Client respondents represented organizations from a variety of industries including financial services, software, technology, engineering services, manufacturing, aerospace, pharmaceuticals, life sciences, healthcare, and other industries (see Figure X.1). Provider and advisor respondents represented organizations of varying sizes. The majority of provider and advisor firms employed fewer than 10,000 employees (see Figure X.2).

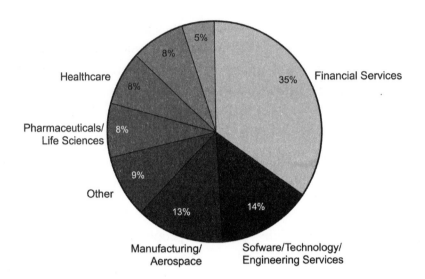

Figure X.1: Client Industries Represented
(n=63 client respondents)

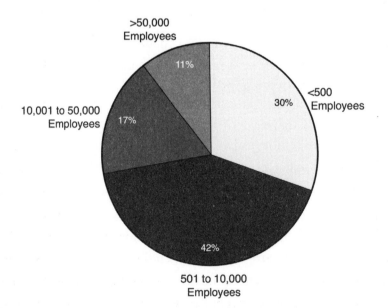

Figure X.2: Size of Provider/Advisor Firms
(n=76)

In February 2016, we repeated the survey at the IAOP world outsourcing summit, when 64 clients, 39 providers and 17 advisors answered a survey administered during the client-only and provider/advisor only networking sessions.[53] Respondents, client industries represented and size of provider/advisers were not that dissimilar to those in 2015. By this date 14 percent of client organizations had adopted RPA, with another 44 percent considering RPA. Meanwhile 13 percent had adopted cognitive automation, and 33 percent were considering CA adoption. These are quite low figures, though it must be pointed out that, according to commentators like Everest Group and Forrester Research, 2016 subsequently saw a revenue growth rate exceeding 100 percent in the combined RPA/CI markets. In 2017 we will conduct two more surveys to assess adoption rates and to benchmark RPA best practices.

Interviews

We needed key participants at the front lines of service automation adoption to answer the research questions: Why do organizations adopt service automation tools? What are their adoption journeys? What outcomes do they achieve? What risks do they face? What action principles explain the outcomes? Key participant interviews were an appropriate method because we sought answers to questions in which the subject matter was sensitive (like any form of automation) and because we were more concerned with the quality, not quantity, of responses.[54] Through 2015-2017, we conducted interviews with 61 people, including 33 people representing 26 client organizations that adopted service automation, 19 people representing 7 providers of service automation tools and services, and 9 advisors with service automation expertise. Interviews occurred in person, over the phone, or over email depending on the availability and preferences of interviewees.

Client interviews

We posed a number of questions to clients pertaining to their service automation adoption, business value delivered, and lessons learned. The specific questions were:

- **Client adoption**: Briefly describe your service automation adoption story within your organization. Did you do a proof-of-concept, and if so, when and on what process? What was your initial business case? What risks did you face? What were the critical success factors?
- **Business value delivered**: How has service automation delivered on the initial business case in terms of financial (i.e. cost savings, return on investment), operational (i.e. improved quality, faster delivery, better compliance), and strategic value (i.e. strategy enablement, access to new customers, better customer retention)?
- **Lessons learned**: What overall lessons did you learn? If you had to do your service automation implementation all over again, what three things would you change? Why?

In total, the client interviewees commented upon 26 service automation adoption stories. We drew upon all interviews, some focused primarily on risk, and list 20 of these from which we could construct a detailed history of the automation journey (see Table X.1). We have permission to name eight of the client organizations. We assigned pseudonyms to the other client organizations.

The majority of client organizations are headquartered in the United Kingdom (UK) or the United States, but we also have adoption stories from companies headquartered in Australia, France, Germany, Sweden, South Africa, Netherlands, and Russia. The client organizations represent 14 industries, illustrating that service automation is not restricted to certain industries. Among the 20 detailed histories, 15 adoptions took place within business operations; only three were led by people from Information Technology (IT) departments, two were lead by a centralized innovation group. Fifteen clients adopted automation technologies that fall within the Realm of RPA, four fall within the realm of cognitive automation, and one client was doing both. The 20 client organizations adopted service automation tools/platforms from Blue Prism (n=10), IBM (n=2), Automation Anywhere (n=2), Infosys (n=1); Automated Insights (n=1), Celaton (n=1), Redwood (n=1); Workfusion (n=1), and IPsoft (n=1).

Company name	Industry	Head-quarters	Adoption location	Realm	First processes automated
1. Ascension MSC	Healthcare	US	BO	RPA	Employee record updates
2. Associated Press	Media	US	BO	RPA	Corporate earnings reports
3. Blue Cross Blue Shield- North Carolina	Healthcare Insurance	US	BO	RPA	Claims processing
4. Biotech	Biotechnology	Netherlands	BO	RPA	Financial close
5. Building Society	Financial Services	UK	BO	RPA	Mortgage lending and savings
6. Consulting	Consulting	France	BO	RPA	Still considering pilot options
7. Deakin University	Higher Education	Australia	BO/IT	CA	Student engagement
8. Energy	Natural Gas	Russia	BO	RPA	New customer registration
9. Financial Services	Financial Services	UK	BO	RPA	Payroll verification
10. Healthcare	Healthcare	UK	BO	RPA	Patient registration
11. Insurance	Insurance Services	UK	IT	RPA	Pension enrolment
12. Professional Services	Professional Services	US	Innovation Center	CA	Commercial Loan grading; Business Development
13. Telefónica O2	Telecommunications	UK	BO	RPA	SIM Swaps; pre-calculated credit
14. Utility	Electric and Gas	Germany	BO	RPA	Meter reading feasibility checks
15. VHA	Healthcare	US	IT	RPA	Web crawls for product descriptions
16. Virgin Trains	Transportation	UK	BO	CA	Incoming customer correspondence
17. Xchanging	BPO Provider	UK	BO	RPA	Premium Advice Notices
18. Manufacturing	Consumer Goods	Germany	BO	RPA	Back Office Processing
19. Bank	Financial Services	South Africa	Innovation Center	RPA/ CA	Credit
20. Bank	Financial services	Sweden	IT	CA	IT service desk

Table X.1: Sample Provider Organizations Represented

Legend: BO = Business Operations; IT = IT Department

Providers Represented

In all, nine provider organizations are represented in the study: Automated Insights, Automation Anywhere, Blue Prism, Celaton, Infosys, IPsoft, Workfusion, IBM and Redwood. The major service automation tools and sample clients of seven of these are listed in Table X.2. The other two are IBM and Workfusion, both focusing on cognitive automation tools, with Workfusion, during late 2016, offering to give away an RPA tool for free.

Service Automation Provider	Service Automation Tool	Service Automation Tool Description	Sample client adopter from our study
1. Automated Insights	Wordsmith	"Generates narratives from structured data and story structures"[55]	The Associated Press
2. Automation Anywhere	AA Enterprise; AA Small Business; AA metabots	"Our software bots run processes and assess information in the way a human would: acting on structured and semi-structured data to automate end-to-end, and gauging sentiment with unique natural language processes."[56]	VHA
3. Blue Prism	Blue Prism	"We provide an enterprise-strength Robotic Process Automation software platform which is robust, highly scalable, powerful and flexible, designed from first principles to provide organizations with a business owned and IT supported Virtual Workforce."[57]	Telefónica O2; Xchanging; Utility
4. Celaton	inSTREAM	"inSTREAM applies artificial intelligence to streamline labour intensive clerical tasks and decision making, and transform the way that organisations handle the unstructured content that flows in every day from customers including correspondence, claims and complaints received by email, social media, fax & post."[58]	Virgin Trains
5. IPsoft	Amelia	"Artificially intelligent cognitive agent"[59] Virtual agent that understands, learns and problem solves within a context of emotional sentiment recognition.[60]	SEB Bank
6. Infosys	Infosys Automation Platform (IAP); Panaya	"We are leveraging AI and knowledge-based techniques to solve ticketing problems with Infosys Automation Platform(IAP)*, automating not merely the business processes but also the experience in BPO, through Panaya* automating application maintenance and application testing."[61]	(Provider interview only)
7. Redwood	RoboClose	"Redwood looks for comprehensive robotization of entire processes, e.g. Record to Report, Procure to Pay and Order to Cash and goes across processes to add value. Rather than communicate with applications at the user interface level (UI) and mimicking user interactions, Redwood robots communicate directly with core ERP and other business systems at the server level (API)."[62]	Royal DSM

Table X.2: Sample Provider Organizations Represented

Because providers are sensitive about what their products are called, we provide a brief overview of how providers describe their service automation tools. Automated Insights positions itself as *an automated content creator* that accesses big data to automatically write narratives from predefined story structures. Its main product is called "Wordsmith". Automation Anywhere positions itself as an *RPA and cognitive technology* provider. As of mid 2016, it had three main products: AA Enterprise, AA Small Business and AA metabots. Blue Prism positions itself as an enterprise *RPA provider*. Blue Prism emphasizes that its product is designed for enterprises and meets strict standards for enterprise security, control, data integrity, change management, scalability, robustness and scheduling. Celaton positions itself as a *cognitive learning technology provider*. Its main product is inSTREAM. The software reads and interprets unstructured and structured textual data. IPsoft has a number of service automation tools, the most interesting perhaps is "Amelia". Amelia is described as an *artificially intelligent cognitive agent* that understands unstructured texts like manuals, learns from 'watching' human agents, and problem solves within a context of emotional sentiment recognition that assesses degree of dominance, arousal, and pleasure.

Infosys, a global leader in consulting, technology, and outsourcing services, has a number of service automation platforms and tools, including Infosys Automation Platform (IAP) and Panaya. In our first book, Pravin Rao, COO, described these tools to us as follows: *"We are leveraging AI and knowledge-based techniques to solve ticketing problems with Infosys Automation Platform (IAP), automating not merely the business processes but also the experience in BPO, through Panaya automating application maintenance and application testing."* Finally, Redwood looks for comprehensive robotization of entire processes, e.g. Record to Report, Procure to Pay and Order to Cash and goes across processes to add value. Rather than communicate with applications at the user interface level (UI) and mimicking user interactions, Redwood robots communicate directly with core ERP and other business systems at the server level (API), allowing greater process standardization, compliance, control, and audit trail. Workfusion and IBM capabilities are slightly outside the remit of this RPA risk mitigation study. Readers are referred to their websites for details of their products and services.

Advisor interviews

We asked nine advisors questions pertaining to client service automation adoption, effects on outsourcing, automation tool capabilities, and the future of work as a consequence of automation. Seven advisor organizations are represented in the study: The Everest Group, KPMG, Ernst and Young, McKinsey, Horses for Sources (HfS), Information Services Group (ISG), and Alsbridge (subsequently bought by ISG).

In addition to these empirical methods, several providers gave product demonstrations and the lead author completed an RPA foundations course to assess the claims about ease of use.

Endnotes

1   Willcocks, L. and Griffiths, C (1998) Management and Risk in Major IT Projects. In Willcocks, L. Feeny, D. and Islei, G. (eds.) *Managing IT As A Strategic Resource.* (McGraw Hill, Maidenhead)

2   Willcocks, L. and Griffiths, C (1998) Management and Risk in Major IT Projects. In Willcocks, L. Feeny, D. and Islei, G. (eds.) *Managing IT As A Strategic Resource.* (McGraw Hill, Maidenhead)

3   Willcocks, L. and Griffiths, C (1998) Management and Risk in Major IT Projects. In Willcocks, L. Feeny, D. and Islei, G. (eds.) *Managing IT As A Strategic Resource.* (McGraw Hill, Maidenhead)

4   Willcocks, L. and Griffiths, C (1998) Management and Risk in Major IT Projects. In Willcocks, L. Feeny, D. and Islei, G. (eds.) *Managing IT As A Strategic Resource.* (McGraw Hill, Maidenhead)

5   Sandman, P. (2017) Introduction and Orientation. http://www.Psandman.com, accessed 12th February 2017.

6   Lacity, M., and Willcocks, L. (2016), A New Approach to Automating Services. *Sloan Management Review*, Vol. 57, 1, pp. 41-49.

7   Lacity, M. and Willcocks, L. (2017), *Service Automation: Cognitive Virtual Agents at SEB Bank*, The LSE Outsourcing Unit ,Working Research Paper Series.

8   Susman, G. and Evered, R. (1978), An Assessment of The Scientific Merits of Action Research, *Administrative Science Quarterly*, 23(4): 582-603.

9   Willcocks, L. and Lacity, M. (2016), *Service Automation: Robots and the Future of Work*. (S.B. Publishing, UK) Available from http://sbpublishing.org/service_automation.html

10 For full case studies of RPA in shared services, see: Lacity, M. and Willcocks, L. (2016), *Robotic Process Automation: The Next Transformation Lever for Shared Services*. The LSE Outsourcing Unit Working Research Paper Series.

11 Presentation on Financial Services: *Enterprise Robotic Process Automation for Banking by BluePrism.*

12 See *CSC Completes Xchanging Acquisition*, press release, May 5, 2016. http://www.csc.com.

13 *ISG Acquires Alsbridge in Transformational Combination; Creates New Powerhouse in Technology Research, Advisory and Digital Transformation Services.* http://www.prnewswire.com/news-releases/isg-acquires-alsbridge-in-transformational-combination-creates-new-powerhouse-in-technology-research-advisory-and-digital-transformation-services-300371828.html

14 See for example: Fersht, P. (2016), *So ISG bought Alsbridge. That happened.* http://www.horsesforsources.com/alsbridge-ISG_120216

[15]   Presentation on Financial Services: *Enterprise Robotic Process Automation for Banking by BluePrism.*

[16]   Presentation on Financial Services: *Enterprise Robotic Process Automation for Banking by BluePrism.*

[17]   Quote from Willcocks, L. and Lacity, M. (2016), *Service Automation: Robots and the Future of Work* (S.B. Publishing, UK) p. 245-246.

[18]   Lacity, M. and Willcocks, L. (2016), *Robotizing Global Financial Shared Services.* The LSE Outsourcing Unit Working Research Paper Series

[19]   Fredrick Brookes first published *The Mythical Man-Month: Essays on Software Engineering* in 1975. He argued that adding more programmers at a software development project merely delays the project further due to the extra time required for onboarding, transferring knowledge and coordinating more people.

[20]   Willcocks, L. and Lacity, M. (2016), *Service Automation: Robots and the Future of Work* (S.B. Publishing, UK) p. 246.

[21]   The Standard Bank story comes from the *HfS webinar* on Wednesday, September 28, 2016 and email input from Ian Weir

[22]   For the entire case study, see Lacity, M. and Willcocks, L. (2016), Robotic Process Automation at Telefónica O2. *MIS Quarterly Executive*, Vol. 15, 1, pp. 21-35

[23]   Quote from Willcocks, L. and Lacity, M. (2016), *Service Automation: Robots and the Future of Work* (S.B. Publishing, UK) p.246.

[24]   Asatiani, A. and Penttinen, E. (2016), *Turning robotic process automation into commercial success – Case OpusCapita.* Journal of Information Technology Teaching Cases, 6(2), pp. 1-8. http://link.springer.com/article/10.1057/jittc.2016.5

[25]   These references show years of research tying senior management support to project success: Standish Group Chaos Report: https://www.infoq.com/articles/standish-chaos-2015; Rajiv Sabherwal, A Jeyaraj, C Chowa, (2006), Information System Success: Individual and Organizational Determinants. *Management Science*, 52 (12): 1849-1864; Lacity, M. (editor), (2008), *Major Currents in Information Systems: The Management of Information Systems*, Volume 4 (series editors: Willcocks, L. and Lee, A.), Sage, London: Nelson, R. (2007), IT Project Management: Infamous Failure, Classic Mistakes, and Best Practices. *MIS Quarterly Executive*, Vol. 6, 2, pp. 67-78.

[26]   Willcocks, L., Lacity, M. and Craig, A. (2015), *Robotic Process Automation at Xchanging*, The LSE Outsourcing Unit Working Research Paper Series

[27]   Dunlap, R. and Lacity, M. (2017), Resolving Tussles in Service Automation Deployments: Service Automation at Blue Cross Blue Shield North Carolina. *Journal of Information Technology Teaching Cases*, Vol. 6, 2

[28]   See Willcocks, L., Cullen, S. and Craig, A. (2011) *The Outsourcing Enterprise: From cost management to collaborative innovation* (Palgrave, London), especially chapter 5 'Collaborating

to Innovate: The next phase.' Also Lacity, M. and Willcocks, L. (2014) *Nine Keys To World Class Business Process Outsourcing* (Bloomsbury, London), especially chapters 8 and 10. Also Cullen, S., Lacity, M. and Willcocks, L. (2014) *Outsourcing – All You Need To Know* (White Plume Publishing, Melbourne). The academic findings are remarkably consistent over many years. See for example Willcocks, L., Feeny, D. and Islei, G. (1997) *Managing IT As A Strategic Resource* (McGraw Hill, Maidenhead), especially chapters 6-10.

[29] Lacity, M. and Willcocks, L. (2013), Beyond Cost Savings: Outsourcing Business Processes for Innovation. *Sloan Management Review*, Vol. 54, 3, pp. 63-69.

[30] Gainsharing at the relationship level establishes targets for the overall performance of the relationship, usually assessed yearly. Clients and providers reported many problems with this gainsharing mechanism. Some clients think gainshare targets are too low and resent when the provider earned the gainshare. Some clients and providers could not agree on a baseline performance measure, resulting in the parties abandoning the notion of gainsharing even though it was designed into the deal. Source: Lacity, M. and Willcocks, L. (2014), Business Process Outsourcing and Dynamic Innovation. *Strategic Outsourcing: An International Journal*, Vol. 7, 1, pp. 66-92.

[31] See *HfS Blueprint: Design Thinking in the As-a-service economy* at https://www.hfsresearch.com/blueprint/hfs-blueprint-design-thinking-service-economy

[32] For more on the role of IT and RPA, see *CIO Magazine* Interview, 'Should CIOs be chief robot wranglers?' July 26, 2016.

[33] Lacity, M. and Willcocks, L. (2016), Robotic Process Automation at Telefónica O2. *MIS Quarterly Executive*, Vol. 15, 1, pp. 21-35.

[34] For an example of a controlled experiment of two service providers, see Lacity, M., Willcocks, L. and Burgess, A. (2014), *The Rise of Legal Services Outsourcing* (Bloomsbury, UK).

[35] See Practice 4 on pages 20-22 in Lacity, M. and Rottman, J. (2008), *Offshore Outsourcing of IT Work* (Palgrave, UK).

[36] Lacity, M. and Fox, J. (2008), Creating Global Shared Services: Lessons from Reuters. *MIS Quarterly Executive* Vol. 7, 1, pp. 17-32.

[37] Dunlap, R. and Lacity, M. (2017), Resolving Tussles in Service Automation Deployments: Service Automation at Blue Cross Blue Shield North Carolina. *Journal of Information Technology Teaching Cases*, Vol. 7.

[38] Discussion from The Robotic Automation Advisory Council, Chicago Illinois, April 14, 2015.

[39] This study summarizes processes suitable for outsourcing: Lacity, M. and Willcocks, P. (2012), *Advanced Outsourcing Practice: Rethinking ITO, BPO, and Cloud Services* (Palgrave, London); This study looks at processes suitable for shared services: McKeen, J. and Smith, H. (2011) Creating IT Shared Services. *Communications of the AIS*, Vol. 29, 34, pp. 645-656.

[40] These studies look at standardization: McIvor, R., McCracken, M. and McHugh, M., (2011) Creating outsourced shared services arrangements: Lessons from the public sector. *European Management Journal*, Vol. 29, 6, pp. 448-461; Sako, M., (2010) Technology Strategy and Management Outsourcing Versus Shared Services. *Communications of the ACM*, Vol. 53, 7, pp. 126-129.

Endnotes

41 For example, see: Srikanth, K. and Puranam, P., (2011) Integrating Distributed Work: Comparing Task Design, Communication, And Tacit Coordination Mechanisms. *Strategic Management Journal*, Vol. 32, 8, pp. 849-875.

42 Bidwell, M., (2012) Politics and Firm Boundaries: How Organizational Structure, Group Interests, and Resources Affect Outsourcing. *Organization Science*, Vol. 23, 6, pp. 1622-1642; Lacity, M., and Fox, J. (2008), Creating Global Shared Services: Lessons from Reuters. *MIS Quarterly Executive*, Vol. 7, 1, pp. 17-32.

43 Panel discussion, 'The Impact of Robotic Process Automation on BPO'. *Automation Innovation Conference*, New York City, December 10, 2014.

44 Presentation 'The Impact of Robotic Process Automation on BPO'. *Automation Innovation Conference*, New York City, December 10, 2014.

45 Von Bertalanffy, L. (1968), General Systems Theory: Foundations, Development and Applications (New York, George Braziller).

46 Lacity, M. and Willcocks, L. (2016), *Robotizing Global Financial Shared Services,* The LSE Outsourcing Unit Working Research Paper Series.

47 Willcocks, L., Feeny, D. and Islei, G. (eds), Managing IT as a Strategic Resource (McGraw Hill, UK).

48 http://www.cvisiontech.com/library/ocr/accurate-ocr/ocr-accuracy-rates.html

49 See for example: Manyika, J. and Chui, M, Miremadi, M. et al. (2017). *A Future That Works: Automation, Employment and Productivity* (McKinsey Global Institute, New York).

50 See for example the estimates from Fersht, P., Snowdon, J., and Reuner, T. (2016), *Automation will trim 1.4 million global services jobs by 2021.* http://www.hfsresearch.com/pointsofview/automation-will-trim-14-million-global-services-jobs-2021

51 https://www.successperformancesolutions.com/65-percent-of-todays-students-will-be-employed-in-jobs-that-dont-exist-yet/

52 The survey results were initially published in Lacity, M., Willcocks, L., and Yan, A. (2015), Are the robots really coming? Service Automation Survey Findings. *Pulse Magazine*, Issue 17, pp. 14-21.

53 Lacity, M. and Willcocks, L. (2016), Speed of Automation Adoption Faster for Providers than Customers. *Pulse Magazine*, May/June, pp. 10-17.

54 These articles discuss the uses and appropriateness of key participant interviews as a research method:

  • Elmendorf, W. and Luloff, A. (2006), Using Key Informant Interviews to Better Understand Open Space Conversation in a Developing Watershed. *Arboriculture & Urban Forestry*, 32, 54-61.

  • Fontana, A., and Frey, J., (1994), Interviewing: The Art of Science. In: *Handbook of Qualitative Research*, Denzin and Lincoln (eds) pp. 361-376 (Sage Publications, Thousand Oaks).

  • Mahoney, C., (1997), Common Qualitative Techniques. In: *User-Friendly Handbook for Mixed Method Evaluations*, Published by the Division of Research, Evaluation and Communication for the National Science Foundation, publication number NSF97-153, 1-17.

- Seidler, J. (1974), On Using Informants: A technique for collecting quantitative data and controlling for measurement error in organizational analysis. *American Sociological Review*, Issue 39, pp. 816-831.
- Yin, R. (2003), Case Study Research: Design and Methods, Third Edition (Sage, Thousand Oaks).

[55] https://automatedinsights.com/blog/introducing-wordsmith-using-data-to-reinvent-how-we-write/

[56] https://www.automationanywhere.com/technology

[57] http://www.blueprism.com/our-products

[58] http://www.celaton.com/

[59] http://www.ipsoft.com/ipsoft-humanizes-artificial-intelligence-with-the-next-generation-of-its-cognitive-agent-amelia/

[60] http://gartner.mediasite.com/Mediasite/Play/97592783dab746279f65898c313046c51d

[61] Email interview with Pravin Rao, COO and Member of the Board, Infosys;

[62] Lacity, M., Willcocks, L. and Craig, A. (2016) *Robotizing Global Financial Shared Services at Royal DSM*, LSE Outsourcing Unit Working Paper.

COMING SOON
February 2018

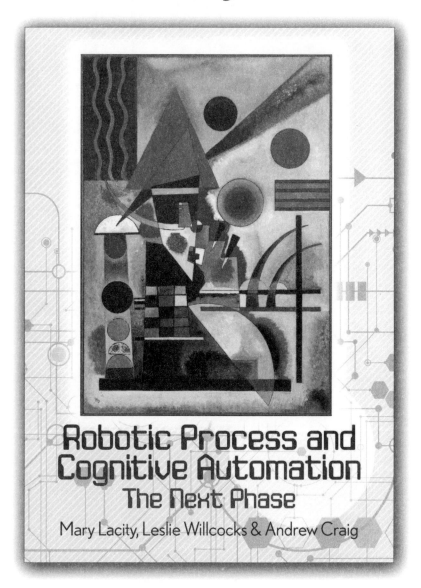

www.roboticandcognitiveautomation.com

Can be pre-ordered from
sbpublishing.org

ISBN 978-0-995682-01-6
worldwide shipping available